Success Secrets for First Time Managers

How to Manage Employees, Meet Your Work Goals, Keep your Boss Happy and Skip the Stress

Matilda Walsh

Table of Contents

Introduction

Congratulations: you made it. You got the job. You are a manager! No matter how many years of hard work, diligence, patience and struggle, you kept going to get to where you are. You have arrived, at last.

Hopefully, you have already cracked open the bubbly and taken a good, long, triumphant sip. You deserve to take the time to bask in this moment, savoring your success. It is important to celebrate success. This is something that great managers do.

Now you have had a moment to take stock—now you have rewarded yourself, quite rightly, for your efforts—it is time to look to the future.

It is time to become a great new manager, the sort who gets it right the first time. Actually, not just the first time: every time. That is what this book is here to teach you.

But being a successful manager brings its own challenges. It is not easy. You know that, because it has been your goal for a while. Maybe you have been working your way up to becoming a manager by climbing the rungs over the months or years in one company. Or, maybe you have been recruited in from elsewhere–so you are not just stepping up to a new role, but find yourself leading a whole new team also. Maybe you applied for a position you never thought you would get, but did. However you got here, what matters is that you made it. Now, the real work begins.

You are about to embark on the challenge of a lifetime, one that, with this book, you stand every chance of rising to. Your new team awaits you. They need you to get this right, right from the start. Happily, you have the right book to help you do this.

The purpose of this book is to empower you to be a great new manager.

Together, we will achieve this in two ways.

First, strategies. In this book are simple, agile, easy, impactful tools that optimize your team. Feasible, flexible, and foolproof, the strategies in this book help you develop a seamless, effective operation. They transform you into the type of manager who gets things right: the work done, the projects delivered, the goals accomplished. The strategies in this book equip you with clear, jargon-free processes and approaches that work from the outset (and work every time).

Second, values. As a great manager, you elevate the people around you. You help your team members meet their own goals, both on a daily basis and for their long term careers. You create a team culture in which people feel appreciated and content. In this way, you generate longevity and stability for your wider organization. The values we explore help you embody success in and beyond your working life.

Everything we study in this book falls under one of these headings: strategies, and values. Sometimes, there is overlap between the two. Effective strategies serve values in the right way. In turn, the right values enrich and strengthen strategies.

The important thing is to master both.

If you can get a grip on both values and strategies, by integrating the advice and approaches contained in this book, you will become a great new manager.

Chapter 1: The Goals of a Manager

As a new manager, you want to get everything right. You want to do this from the beginning—not after months, even years, of trial and error. Getting it right the first time, and every time, is a tall order.

But what, exactly, are you aiming to get right? After all, that is what has brought you to this book. To know that, you must be able to answer one fundamental question: what does a manager do? The simple answer to that question is: managing.

Well, I hear you say. Sure. Managers manage. If they are not managing, they are not getting it right. What is the point here? What are we managing, now that we are new or first-time managers? What are our goals? More importantly, why are these goals our goals?

No matter what sector, industry, or profession you are managing in, and no matter how big or small your organization, managers have two aims:

- To deliver on time, on budget, and to a high standard.
- Manage a team promoting happiness, pride, enabling accomplishments and longevity.

A manager who meets both of these goals is getting it right. This book guides you to meet both aims, teaching you to deliver projects (using strategies) and manage your team (using values).

At the end of each chapter, this book asks you to review what you have learned. It is important to complete the review immediately after finishing each chapter. This promotes better understanding and makes these lessons easier to remember in the years ahead.

There are no answers to the reviews in this book. Like the book itself, the questions are designed to make you think. Some of them are open-ended, intended to provoke reflection and self-improvement. If you cannot come up with an answer to a review question, simply return to the chapter to find it.

Chapter One: Review

Now that you are a manager, what are your two goals?

_____

_____

What will you use to achieve these two goals?

_____

_____

List three values that are important to you in your new role

1. _____
2. _____
3. _____

List three strategies you have used (if you are a first-time manager, list strategies you have used to manage your career progression so far or personal life)

_____

_____

Did these strategies succeed? Why?

_____

_____

Chapter 2: What Makes a Great Manager?

When we reach a position of authority, it is natural to begin to second-guess ourselves. Too often the voice in our head intervenes. You might question whether it is possible to become the great manager envisioned in this book—the manager who gets it right, straight off the bat, and beyond.

It is possible. Yet first you need to know what a great manager is.

To begin, being a great manager is not the same as being a good manager. Moreover, it is definitely not the same as simply not being bad.

To start to grasp the difference between great, good, and bad, ask a friend to tell you about a good manager they know. Chances are, they will be able to mention someone. We have all encountered a good manager, at one point or another in our working lives. We can remember that person. Perhaps we thought they were pretty good, or not bad. For even if we have not had the fortune to work under a decent manager, we still know more or less what one should look like. Good managers do not get angry. They are never rude. They do not interrupt. They do not make unreasonable demands on us, especially on our time. They might even make us feel appreciated sometimes, if only in a small way. In short, they are not bad managers.

If you ask your friend to tell you about a bad manager, they will probably talk your ear off.

Sadly, in this world bad managers are as commonplace as bad coffee. Like really bad coffee, bad managers are bitter. They leave a nasty taste in your mouth when you are done with them. They are just not good, and yet somehow they still continue to make money—even when better alternatives are available. Bad managers, bad coffee: neither is good.

To take this analogy a step further, good coffee is not great coffee. It is not bad, but not great. In the same way, good managers definitely do not do the things that bad managers do. That does not make them great managers. Great managers are something else.

Good managers do not necessarily get it right the first time. What is more, they definitely do not get it right every time. Yet great managers do.

Great managers embody values that empower communication. They wield strategies that ensure success.

In the below sections, we will look at *communicating for greatness*, which rests on values, and *using systems that serve*, which employs strategies.

Communicating for greatness

Great managers communicate for greatness. That means:

- Communicating to empower individuals
- Communicating to elevate the whole team

- Communicating to generate respect in all directions

Set out in this way, it looks quite easy. Actually, it is easy.

Don't worry if you are thinking now that this sounds impossible. If all of us were perfect in all of our interactions all of the time, maybe we would communicate for greatness too. Yet we are not perfect. If we were, we would get our communication right every time. Would we?

Not really.

Getting communication right every time is not the same as being perfect, as you will be relieved to learn. In fact, communicating for greatness leaves plenty of room for our natural, and entirely human, margin of error.

We all make mistakes. We might make twenty or thirty errors of judgment in our communication each and every day—on a normal, not-so-bad day, that is.

We are not super human. We will never become super human, not even now that we are managers. The greatest manager in the world is still a human being, who makes plenty of mistakes, like everybody else.

Yet great managers get communication right in all sorts of ways—including knowing how to be in the wrong. Being wrong is not a problem. Great managers know this. Actually, being wrong in front of the people you manage, and knowing how to handle it, is an opportunity for honesty, humbleness, and growth—for all the team. Being wrong in the right way is just one of the ways in which you can *communicate for greatness*.

So now that we have got that out of the way, let me reassure you that it is easy to get communication right when you know how. It does not necessitate perfection. It merely means knowing what to aim at in every interaction. It involves knowing how to be—how to set out to be, in any case. There are simple tricks and tips to empower you, as a new manager, to do just this.

With that cleared up, let us take a look at how to get your communication right the first time—and every time—by communicating for greatness.

Being aware

Communicating for greatness involves being aware.

Awareness, in the context of communication, goes far beyond paying attention. It encompasses a proper focus on the interaction in question, on your part in it, and on other people's parts in it, too.

Many business books claim to teach you how to be a "great listener". However, they seldom mention the things you need to get right first—the conditions you need to create for every interaction with your team members. Essentially, these are the conditions you need to create in your communications so that you can *be aware*.

Here is how to get the groundwork right:

If you are available to communicate, be available to communicate: always. You must be fully available at those times when your team knows you are available. That is not all the time. For more on setting boundaries to optimize communication, see *Being Present* below.

Be willing to listen: always. You cannot pay attention to people if your awareness is elsewhere. When someone comes to speak to you in person, lock your PC. Or, close your laptop. Turn to face the person speaking to you.

Do this before you know what they want from you and whether it is important: always. It sounds counter-intuitive, but it really works. When the people you manage know that they will get your attention when they need it, they soon stop bothering you over small things.

Listening to people

People communicate for all kinds of purposes, in and out of the workplace. Saying "No, thank you" to a partner, spouse, sibling, boss, or subordinate, can carry with it a whole range of intentions and inflections. As managers, we cannot limit listening to the words we hear. We have to listen "around" the words, too, and lean into the context. We have to be aware of what is unsaid, as much as what is made explicit.

Making the people you manage feel understood is of fundamental importance. At work, people communicate to express emotions, as well as to resolve and explore practical considerations. Hearing what they have to say is all fine and good. Any business manual will advise you to hear your team by:

- Maintaining eye contact
- Nodding; making noises of assent; giving other visual aids to demonstrate understanding
- Repeating anything you have not understood, or anything especially emotive, using language like "So what I am hearing you say is..." and "So, I sense that you feel that..."
- Not interrupting the person
- Maintaining a neutral or positive facial expression throughout the interaction

- Asking questions appropriately and at the right moment

 What business manuals don't teach you is how to understand the person you manage when they are speaking to you. Understanding involves everything on the list above. Yet that is just the start.

The recommendations recounted above probably are quite familiar to you. In truth, in practice they often come off as formulaic—both for the listener and the person being listened to. These days, people recognize the tips, tricks, and hacks that every business manual spouts on the subject of effective communication and emotional intelligence. If you simply follow the list, and fail to do anything beyond it to understand your team, the individuals will know that you are just "being a good listener". At worst, they might even find it a little phony, especially if you adopt phrases that are not natural to you, your personality, or management style.

Understanding your team

Understanding a person you manage is different to listening to them and hearing them out.

Understanding includes filling in a broader picture around that person and their communications.

It means fleshing out the context of the conversation, so that you know what your team member wants to achieve in the interaction.

When people approach managers, sometimes they want something from you. More often, they want to tell you that they have done something: something right, something wrong, something on time. Or, they tell you about the thing they have not done, not yet, but will do soon. Sometimes, they simply want to have a moan. A lot of the time, they want to connect with you, impress you, tell you something about them, or simply share a remark about the upcoming weekend.

It really does not matter what your team member says. Great managers know how to understand the people they manage—in every interaction. When you understand a person, you know if you can help them achieve the aims of that conversation. Then, you can respond appropriately.

To understand the person, you should follow these steps:

- Think about what you know of this person's day so far. What is their role? With whom do they work closely? What implications does that have? What is their schedule like? Do they have deadlines soon?
- Think about what you know about this person's life outside of work. And if you do not know all that much, how and when can you change this?
- Ask yourself how the person might be feeling right now. How do they seem today, compared to other days?
- Finally, assess whether how they are feeling matches what they are saying.

When you run through these four steps throughout your interactions, you go beyond merely listening to people. Instead, you understand your team members. You actively consider the context of what you are hearing them say, as well as the content of their communications. Then, equipped with understanding, you can respond in the right way each time.

Being present—the right amount

If you are going to be aware throughout your daily communications, paying attention properly, as we have seen, and creating a culture of listening and understanding, then you are going to need to be present.

Being present is somewhat of a buzzword nowadays. People use it, loosely and interchangeably, to refer to:

- Being empathetic
- Being mindful

- Being proactive
- Being impactful ("having presence")

Finally, in the world of business, *being present* is also associated with the less laudable concept of *presenteeism*: being the last to leave the office, the first to arrive.

After all, if you master being aware, listening to people, and understanding your team, empathy and mindfulness are par for the course. They are just some of the values that make you a great manager. As for being proactive and impactful, we teach you that in the section on using systems that serve (not serving the systems). In that section, we will look at the strategies that set you apart as a manager and ensure your success.

In this book, *being present* is not any of these things. Instead, it refers to communicating to your team *exactly how and when you are available to communicate.* It is an essential component of communicating for greatness.

If you are going to be a great manager the first time, and every time, by listening to people, understanding them, and being aware, it is going to take quite a bit of your time and energy. There will be times when you can do this and do it justice—*being present*—and times when you will be focusing on crucial tasks, outside of communicating with your team. It is reasonable, and advisable, to set clear boundaries and frameworks for when you will, and will not, be present to communicate with the people you manage. All you have to do is... communicate it.

In fact, setting boundaries for *being present* frees you up to be more present. There have to be times when you cannot communicate, because you have many responsibilities as a manager.

Here is how to set boundaries around communication and *be present*—the right way:

- When you meet your new team, lead with how you will communicate with them.
- Explain what you know about communicating for greatness. Inform them that, together, through communicating in this way, your team will enjoy collective and individual successes.

- Elaborate on how you will listen to them and understand them.
- State that you are aware when you interact with people. Show them how you do this.
- Explain that you cannot do this every hour of the working week, else communication will fail and take the team with it.
- Detail the times, places, and ways in which you will or will not *be present* to communicate.
- It does not matter whether your business setting is remote, hybrid, or on site. *Being present* works the same way.

As you know, great managers have great values. Values can never be separated from communication. That is why this book has begun with an in-depth study of how to *communicate for greatness*.

Values are spread, fed, and shaped by great interactions and great communicators. If you use awareness, listening, understanding, and presence, your team needs to know it. They need to value it.

When your team values what you value, successes abound.

Now that you have mastered *communicating for greatness,* let us turn our attention to the value that underlies everything we have learned so far.

Integrity

Great managers are great people. They are consistent. They follow through. They are congruent, honest, and fair. They are accountable, transparent, dependable, and responsible. They think of others. They have integrity.

Integrity is not taught. Arguably, claiming to teach integrity in a book would itself lack integrity.

Yet it is valuable, at this juncture, to reflect on yourself and the notion of integrity.

The exercise below is designed to help you to recognize the hallmarks of integrity in yourself and in others.

You should do this activity three times, at three month intervals. Then, you should return in ninety days' time to fill out the second column. Finally, you should return to the exercise a third time to see what the value of integrity means to you—six months into your new life as a manager.

Exercise: The Hallmarks of Integrity

Today / 3 months / 6 months

❖ "I do not know the answer to that."

a. Managers use this phrase

i. too much
ii. not enough
iii. the right amount

b. I use this phrase

i. too much
ii. not enough

iii. the right amount

❖ "Maybe you're right."

c. This phrase

i. has integrity
ii. lacks integrity
because_____

d. I use this phrase

i. too much
ii. not enough
iii. the right amount

❖ "That would go against our values."

e. This phrase
i. has integrity
ii. lacks integrity
because_____

f. Managers use this phrase

i. too much

ii. not enough

iii. the right amount

❖ "That would go against my beliefs."

g. This phrase

i. has integrity

ii. lacks integrity

because_____

h. Managers should use this phrase

i. only rarely

ii. sometimes

iii. as often as it applies

❖ "Right now, I feel…"

i. This phrase

i. has integrity

ii. lacks integrity

because_____

j.   I use this phrase

i. rarely
ii. often

k.   Managers should use this phrase

i. only rarely
ii. sometimes
iii. as often as it applies

❖ "I know you were promised x, but actually…"

l.   Managers should use this phrase

i. never
ii. sometimes
iii. Frequently
because_____

❖ "This was a really difficult decision and it causes me pain."

m. Managers should use this phrase

i. rarely

ii. sometimes

iii. as often as it applies

because_____

Using systems that serve success

Now you have learned the importance of *communicating for greatness* as the foundation of your values, underpinned by *integrity*, it is time to explore the strategies and systems that *serve success*.

The fundamental thread running through the systems we teach in this book is that they serve you—not the other way around.

As you read the recommendations below, ask yourself if each tip is something you could try. If it is feasible for your working context and style, you could give it a try. Yet you must not become wedded to any one system just for the sake of it. If you fall into that trap, you will end up serving the systems—rather than wielding them for your success as a manager.

It is advisable to think of this section as your buffet menu. Like visiting the buffet, not everything in the smorgasbord of strategies below will suit your tastes as a manager.

Pick and mix from the tips below to create a plateful of bespoke strategies that systematize the right way. Highlight, annotate, scribble, or bookmark the systems that appeal to you particularly. Then, trial the system at work for as long as it works for you. If it stops working, stop using it: immediately. You can always come back to the list and try something new.

Organization & multi-tasking

Digital team calendar. It does not matter what software you use. Just ensure that it is synced to all devices and available for your team to view at all times. Delegate this. Never use the digital team calendar for personal appointments or sensitive business meetings.

Agile analogue diary—for anything you do not wish the team as a whole to see.

The best analogue diaries are tailored to you. You might use a bullet journal, or some other flexible system. A favorite system of a great manager I knew was the Filofax Refillable Notebook. A fantastic customizable diary option, all the pages clip out. Refills can be purchased from Filofax as required. This diary comes with divider tabs, letting you organize it by sections. However, the small post-its used to mark pages in novels would work just fine instead. Then, you have sections for the diverse areas of managerial life: meetings, appraisals, projects, notes, ideas, personal career goals, memos.

Visual organizers/mind-mappers. No matter what sector you operate in, workspaces are vastly improved by pinboards, moodboards, whiteboards, and the good old-fashioned blackboard. Not everyone is a visual thinker, but there will be at least one among the people you manage. Make a statement in your office by placing an appealing visual device in a prominent position. For remote workspaces, digital equivalents abound.

Workflow systems. Much of this will depend on any existing systems used in your organization. If your company is small, there may be scope to transform your team's workflow easily. In larger companies, there could be resistance. Make it your business to ask your team members if the current workflow system works for them. Review any project management system already in place, asking yourself—and others—if there are areas of the workflow system that are being used just for the sake of it. If so, your team is serving the system and you need to change it.

Also, ask yourself if the existing workflow system has any capabilities that are not fully exploited by your team. Ask yourself and the people you manage if that should change.

Inbox systems. Everyone has their own system for managing an inbox. What works for one person might not work for another. The important thing to note is this: now that you are a manager, you are entering a whole new world of inbox intensity. Prepare to receive more emails in a week than you have had hot dinners.

Faced with the avalanche of emails you are about to receive, you will probably experience a moment of empathy for the most stressed-out manager you ever had the misfortune to meet. Happily, you do not have to be that manager. All you need to do is find the right system for your inbox.

Let us get one thing straight: no system does not work. It may have worked for you when you were not a manager. It will not work for you now. You need to get your inbox system sorted.

Mailboxes have a range of tools these days to prioritize and organize tasks and emails. Some managers like to create folders for emails and file everything that has been resolved, leaving only outstanding queries in their inbox.

Others prefer to color-code their inbox, opting for a visual system where all email communications are a click away.

Some use the priority function, or pin anything pressing to the top of their mailbox.

Many managers like to keep a record of their own responses, bcc-ing themselves into all emails and filing accordingly. It saves scrolling through long threads.

Any of these, and any combination, could work for you.

Problem-solving systems (solution systems)

Naturally, as great new managers we are focused on solutions: not problems. You will learn about this in Chapter Four, where we will explore how to survey problematic situations and design strategies to ameliorate them.

However, it is often useful to have some *practical strategies to explore solutions to the problems you are managing*. There are many systems that you can use to do this.

First off, if you are a structured and systematic thinker, mind-mapping out the potential solutions can assist you. The good old-fashioned spider diagram goes a long way here. Colors can again reflect the different factors of the problem and facets of the solutions.

On the other hand, you could consider a more creative approach. Why not try drawing the problem? It sounds like the stuff of schoolchildren, yet it is not to be dismissed. Neuroscience has established that so-called "right brain activities" (e.g. creative and ludic pursuits: poetry, performing arts, playing games) has benefits for short- and long-term brain health. It is a destructive fallacy that being a good manager is synonymous with being "serious": far from it. Finding creative ways to engage with work problems is good for you and good for your team, too.

You can read more about the playful side of your new role in Chapters Nine and Ten, which explore creating a culture and sparking team spirit.

Detailed-oriented systems

When it comes to detail, the quote attributed to Peter Drucker—"you cannot improve what you do not measure"—says it all.

As a new manager for your team, there will be many things to scope out, assess, review, and reconfigure. The inputs will be complex and manifold.

Sadly, when it comes to detail there are no shortcuts: there is no elegant, one-size-fits-all system to ride in and sweep up the devilish detail into a single structure. If you try to do that, you will end up simplifying things that are not simple.

So, you are going to need some detail-oriented strategies for the nitty gritty. What is more, you will need to adopt a range of detailed systems for your own management purposes. Trial, error, and persistence will be key.

What follows is a list of common detail-oriented systems for appropriately measuring the complexities of your working environment. Realistically, you will use many of these in your new role as a manager. It is up to you to reassess them regularly, so as to ensure you remain agile, solutions-oriented, efficient, and productive.

Spreadsheets.

Microsoft Excel should not be used for everything, but when it comes to financial analysis it remains the powerhouse of the market.

Job costing software.

We have touched briefly on workflow software, yet naturally if your role involves measuring profitability—and few managerial roles do not require this—you will need to use software to track time, materials, margins, profits, and costs, too.
While your company might have an established software solution for this purpose, it is up to you to check that it is serving the needs of the team and the wider company adequately. If it is not, then you need to look at changing the software.

More commonly, you will find that by investing time in learning about using your company's job costing software solution, you can optimize its usage in your team environment.

Performance management.

Although we dive deeply into the subject in Chapter Seven, it is worth noting at this juncture that systems for performance management must be detailed, accurate, comprehensive, and private.

If your company has no such system, it is your responsibility to create one. After all, taking responsibility is what great managers do.

Learning.

Having reached the echelons of management—and having set out to get it right from the very first—you are not going to rest on your laurels or coast. Instead, you are going to continue to grow as a manager. That means that you will continue to learn and develop.

You need to measure your own progress, too. So, you will need a system for this. Failure to learn and measure your growth will serve neither your career, nor your happiness, nor your success. For now, simply be aware that learning is part of your job as a great manager and that you need to track your own learning.

A diary or document to record significant learning events and insights is one way you can do this.

Chapter Two: Review

- List four components of *communicating for greatness.*

1. [Being aware]
2. [Listening to people]
3. [Understanding your team]
4. [Being present]

- Describe three things that strike you about *communicating for greatness.*

_____

_____

_____

- Give a definition of integrity.

_____

_____

_____

- Sort the following into two columns:

Values	Strategies

Awareness   *Problem-solving*

Understanding   *Multi-tasking*

Organization   *Honesty*

Delegation   *Listening*

Systems Accountability

- List three systems you will use this month at work.

_____

_____

_____

- How will you know if you should stop, or continue, using these systems?

_____

- Think about your life outside of being a manager.

Detail a system you have used successfully in order to

a. Manage your time

b. Know where you needed to be and when

c. Record important notes and reflections

d. Change something about yourself

e. Generate creative ideas

f. Plan projects

g. Collaborate on projects

a. _____

b. _____

c. _____

d. _____

e. _____

f. _____

g. _____

- List three so-called "right brain activities".

  _____

  _____

  _____

Chapter 3: Taking Your Team from Tired to Inspired

As a new manager, you are bound to be a bundle of energy. It is important for a great manager to maintain positivity and enthusiasm.

Yet what happens to you—the upbeat new manager, armed with great communication skills, all the right values, and the sharpest strategies in the book— when you bounce into your team's first meeting full of energy, but are met with blank stares and less than enthusiastic responses?

Unfortunately, bad managers exist. Your team might expect you to be one of them. It is going to take some of them some time to warm up to you, trust you, and realize that you walk the walk of great values and strategies, rather than merely talking.

Yet, let us pause to reflect more deeply on where we stand. America has had a couple of years like no other. In the Covid-19 pandemic, we endured stress and upheavals on a scale far beyond anything in our recent memory. We are battleworn and tired. The changes to everyone's working lives, as in our own personal lives, were swingeing and relentless. The aftershocks are still being felt. As a result, cases of workplace burnout are on the rise. People are still in the process of working out how work looks for them and how they feel about this. It has been exhausting. This is the context that you must manage.

Meanwhile, the global economy is challenged by crises as vast and diverse as environmental catastrophe and supply chain chaos. The effects ripple down to you and the people in your team. It is not easy for anyone.

As a result of our experiences, personal or collective, your team members need you to lead with trust and care.

With all of that in mind, let me share the superpowers that inspire a tired, jaded team. These are abilities that, embodied in you as a manager, encourage trust and elevate your team for success.

Approachability

Approachable managers gain trust and respect right off the bat. They do this by doing the dirty work. They take time to get to grips with the tasks performed by all members of the team and they have a go at all of these tasks—at least once.

When employees see that a manager is willing to walk in their shoes, they see a manager who does not merely talk the talk.

Yet it is unrealistic to think that you will be able to accomplish the above for every team member in your first week. Instead, let them know that you will be spending time with each individually over the weeks ahead. Tell them why you do it: you want to understand their role, because they know it and you do not. You cannot manage what you do not understand. Explain this to your team and already they will see you as an approachable manager.

Sometimes, a soft sell works as well as the more obvious, boots-on-the-ground strategy above. If you have an in-person work place, simply setting a jar of candy or toffee on your desk can invite trust from your team. It is up to you whether you wish to offer out the candies or simply label the jar: EAT ME. Either way, you build trust in a fun, approachable way.

Relatability

Approachability helps to give you a second managerial superpower: relatability.

It is the natural counterpoint to being approachable. When you are relatable, your team members can put themselves in your shoes—just like you put yourself in theirs. Ultimately, it means they can imagine being in your position and becoming managers themselves one day. After all, empowering the people around us is one of our values.

Relatable managers give truthful, appropriate information about themselves to their team members at the right moment and in the right way. Because they have *integrity*, and admit their mistakes when they are wrong, people know that these managers are honest in what they say. Demonstrating your personality, humility, and humanity, is an important and powerful trait for you as a leader.

Naturally, you cannot do this all the time. Yet there are ways of incorporating it seamlessly into your very first day as a manager. For instance, you could use an icebreaker to make your relatability known. One favorite is *two truths and a lie*. In this game, you give three statements about your life, one of which is false, and ask your coworkers to guess the lie. In turn, they can tell two truths and a lie about themselves, too. It guarantees a laugh.

Relatable managers use humor. The icebreaker suggested here is just one way of doing that.

Feasibility

Great managers shoot for the stars, all the while ensuring that getting there remains feasible.

It is important to grasp the difference between high expectations and unrealistic goals. What appears a lofty objective to you might seem impossible to a disaffected team member. People bolt when aims and claims come across as overly ambitious—even when these are sincerely felt.

To avoid this pitfall, pair your high expectations with high support.

To create a culture where your team knows that great success is feasible, let them know how you will support them. This could involve many things, from regular one-to-ones to training and upskilling initiatives.

For now, just know that supporting your team to achieve feasible goals requires you to use *processes*. When people know there is a process for getting from A to B, they stop worrying about the feasibility and start to trust.

Sociability

As a new manager, much is within your reach. Yet there are so many things outside of your individual control.

One example—often overlooked—is that of your team's dynamic. Human beings are social creatures. We do not cease to be social when we arrive at work. We do not re-enter our identities as social beings upon leaving the office for the day. We are built for relationships. We relate all the time. When two or more human beings get together, their sociability immediately creates a dynamic.

Dynamics are overwhelming sometimes. The culture of a team, with all its interlinks, internal strengths, weaknesses, and tensions, is a whole far greater than the sum of its parts. All relationships are like this. For proof of this, think of any marriage.

Yet while you can no more control the personalities that comprise your team than you can manipulate the moon or stop the tides, you can influence its dynamic in subtle, yet impactful, ways.

One powerful method to alter team dynamics is to interweave group and individual praise with the simple sandwich approach. When your team deserves credit, shout out at your next meeting. Thank the team as a whole, then name the specific individuals. Then, thank the whole team again. The sandwich effect of thanking the group, then individuals, then the group, reinforces the message of "all for one, and one for all". It contributes to a culture of generous praise and collective success.

Another equally powerful method is to feed into a spirit of competition. Pit your team against another group in the company and you will be surprised at the fire it ignites in the mildest of folk you manage.

Even better, divide your team into mini-teams and hold a weekly contest, sweepstake, or points-for-prizes system.

It is better to celebrate success daily and weekly, with small rewards, than to award one large prize at the end of the quarter.

Regular perks, and a streak of healthy competition, breed a positive, energetic group dynamic for all.

Chapter Three: Review

Categorize the activities that promote, or demonstrate, *relatability, approachability, sociability,* and *feasibility.* You can even add your own ideas, too.

Anecdotes   *Team-building activities*
       Ice-breakers
Inter-team contests   *Intra-team contests*
    The candy jar
Doing the dirty work   *High support*
    Humor   *Truthfulness Sandwiching praise*   *Humanity*   *Humility*
    Training and upskilling   *One-to-ones*

Chapter 4: Working with Your Own Manager

It feels great to step into your new role as a manager. It is exciting to have a team to manage, empower, elevate, and inspire. Yet be under no illusions: you still have your own manager.

Probably, you will always have a manager. Even CEOs in the largest multinationals are accountable to shareholders. That is just the way of the world. It has not altered simply because you have become a manager.

Your new manager might be someone you know well. You might have established a positive working relationship with them already. If that is the case, you are in a strong position to build on that thriving connection to ensure your success for the future. On the other hand, your new manager could be relatively, or completely, new to you. Your working relationship might be neutral, or non-existent, if they are an unknown quantity. In the worst cases, they might just be one of those bad managers.

Moreover, even if you end up getting on with your new manager like a house on fire, there is one potential problem: they might not have read this book. For if that is the case, then you are already a better manager than they are. That can be a thorny issue when you are being managed.

Thankfully, there are ways to manage your manager without them realizing. These strategies center on solutions, not problems. They teach you to manage your manager's expectations—the right way.

Managing your manager's expectations

People are complicated. Managers are no exception. After all, your new manager could be good or bad. Or, if they have read this book, they could be great. You have no control over this.

Starting in your new role as a manager can bring with it some weighty expectations. Some of the pressure you are feeling could even be self-generated, which is not necessarily bad: great managers want to get things right for their team and for themselves. You could also be feeling the impact of your new manager's expectations, both implicit and explicit. You know, having studied communicating for greatness, that so much of human interaction is about what is unsaid—about all the things that are "around" what is communicated. Unspoken expectations can be part of this. They can be hard to manage... unless you know how.

The section below lists ten top tips and approaches for getting things right with your own manager, straight off the bat. Using the strategies that follow, you will be able to manage your manager's expectations effectively and lay the groundwork for a mutually beneficial working relationship for both of you.

Three top tips

1. *Prepare to meet your manager: build a picture of your manager before your first day*

Great managers come prepared.

Using everything you know about your new manager, you should map out what they are like and anticipate how your relationship will be—*before you even start working together*. You should set aside time to do this, along with all your other preparations.

Next, scope out what you know about your manager. What is their professional background? How long have they been a manager for? Do they have a public LinkedIn account and, if so, and if appropriate, can you find out more from there? What about their history at the company so far?

If you do not have much explicit information, you might consider implicit factors. In other words: what can you guess about your new manager? What might their own career goals be? How much do they earn, in your assessment? Demographically, what can you tell about them? What do you know about their personal life and what can you infer from this? It is crucial to see your own manager as a whole person, not just the people whom you manage.

Set the information from your assessment out in a way that makes sense to you. This will create a picture of them. Then, you can start to gauge what they will want from you.

Even if you have already started working for your new manager, you can still undertake this process. Either way, it will help you to understand your manager better.

If you need a tool to help with this, go back to Chapter Two and select an appropriate idea from the section called "Using systems that serve success".

2. *Next, get off to a great start: let your manager manage you*

Having digested the wisdom of this book, starting out in your new role as a great first-time or new manager—equipped with all the necessary strategies and values to drive success and create a happy, worthy working culture—you are going to be enthusiastic. That is quite right.

Yet, please: do not allow your enthusiasm to tip into assertiveness.

Your manager manages you. That is their job. To get off to a good start with your new superior, you need to let them do that job. In other words, they are in charge. You are not going to swan into your new role and ride roughshod over their authority. Pay due respect to their experience and their station. Be self-effacing. Speak less, listen more. Do what they ask you to do, even if you can see a better way already. Allow them to lead.

If you defer to your manager, even when they are wrong, you are getting it right. As a great manager, you understand that effecting change takes time, effort, and care.

As you know, so much of that care is about relationships.

When you let your manager manage you, you empower them and build trust. If your manager does not feel empowered—if their feathers are ruffled— then there will be no trust, no relationship, no communication, no success, and certainly no greatness.

3. Build healthy boundaries

Letting your manager manage you the right way involves building healthy boundaries.

Just as you set clear expectations to your team members regarding *being available,* you must do this with your own manager. Truly, it does not matter if the person in question is your superior or subordinate.

Without healthy boundaries, your manager will not be your manager: they will be your boss.

When you have healthy boundaries with your manager, you encourage them to have the same.

If ever you question whether a boundary has been overstepped, take yourself to a quiet place if possible. Then, make a well-judged, fair assessment of what is or is not feasible or desirable for you and your team. Finally, communicate this to your manager. Healthy boundary-setting is as simple as that.

Managers with healthy boundaries enjoy a better work-life balance. They have better working relationships with their team and with their superiors. They are successful. They know the difference between being managed and being bossed about. They are aware of what is reasonable and what is not—for themselves and for the people around them.

If you adopt these three top tips as your core tenets for interacting with your new manager, you will go beyond their expectations. You will build a positive relationship that serves you, your goals, and those of your team and company.

Finally, you will be excellently positioned to manage that other mainstay of working life: problems.

Managing problems by creating solutions— the right way

Problems intensify when we focus on problems. That might sound obvious to you. Or, it might seem confusing. In any case, it is true. Reframing problems empowers the people you manage and helps to drive change.

As such, the word "problem" is not in a great manager's vocabulary. Rather, your chief friend in troubled times is the word "solution".

Yet make no mistake: this is not about blue sky thinking or burying your head in the sand. Focusing on solutions is not the same as pretending that problems do not exist... far from it.

To break this down, we need to revisit that old cliche of management theory: "Do not bring me problems, bring me solutions".

First off, let us admit that this phrase is a very bad one. It is hackneyed and generic. What is more, it is really quite rude. It is completely unrealistic, and indeed inappropriate, for managers to expect their team members to "bring" the solutions. This insidious phrase divests managers of their rightful duties and leadership role, pushing responsibility for problems back onto the people they manage. Obviously, only bad managers do that.

In fact, managing problems and creating solutions is the job of a great manager. Accepting the inevitability of problems is your job, too. After all, as a new manager, you must know that from day one with your new team there will be adversity. You have to accept that there will be a myriad of issues, big and small, urgent and less pressing, with which you will have to contend daily, weekly, and sometimes hourly. You need to understand that things will go wrong. Moreover, during a particularly unlucky or difficult patch, things might seem as if they never go right. Great managers do not deny the reality of adversity. Adversity is part of life.

Rather, great managers take problems on the chin and, from careful assessment and excellent communication, they create solutions.

Again, much rests on the power of *communicating for greatness*. When great managers choose to apply their awareness to how they engage with problems—focusing carefully on the words they choose and the strategies they use—they reposition themselves as a force for resolving issues and effecting change. When managers use the word "problem", however, they feed into a narrative of disempowerment that serves neither their leadership nor their team and the wider company.

Great managers do not engage with the word "problem", because they know that it quickly descends down rabbit holes into negativity, complaining, lethargy, and other enemies to productivity. They acknowledge that things need to work better; then, they focus positively on ameliorating the situation for all.

Crucially, using positive words and productive strategies to dispel problems and create solutions takes time, research, and reflection. As we have seen, empty or tokenistic optimism is a band-aid— not a solution. Solutions must be underscored by the careful consideration and assessment of the problem in question. Then, the problem can be reframed; solutions can be found and adversity overcome. Great managers do this thoroughly and correctly.

By way of illustration, let us use a scenario.

The following case study is divided into two parts. Part I sets out the scene in some detail, allowing you to survey the problem. Then, there is an activity to complete. This activity is designed to help you gauge how to *manage problems* and *create solutions*. You should thus read all the information in the case study with care. Part II then ensues. Next, there is an opportunity for reflection and self-assessment. A summary then concludes the case study.

I would recommend undertaking the case study in a single session. This will ensure the information remains fresh and salient.

Please note, however, that the case study below is followed by the customary chapter review. So, you could consider building in a break between undertaking the case study and the chapter review.

Case study: Surveying the problem, designing the solution

Part I

Rachel has been recruited externally to manage a team of administrators. The company performs building surveying for retail and commercial clients. However, the business is currently merging with an architectural consultancy. They are modern, technologically-savvy, and ambitious. The architects are high fee earners. Pressure is on the building surveyors to step up. Change is afoot and efficiency is the watchword.

The surveying arm of the company—Rachel's domain—presently uses a number of antiquated practices. These are not working well. They are causing huge inefficiencies for both the administrative and client-facing sides of the surveying business, resulting in unacceptable delays in delivering projects for clients. Customers are growing angry, because the building survey reports for the properties they wish to purchase are taking four or five weeks to generate: the target is ten days.

Rachel's manager Robert, the lead surveyor, needs Rachel's team to resolve the backlog urgently. On Rachel's first day, he greeted her briefly and then described the situation, using the words: "This is a serious problem. We need you to fix it now."

Rachel has spent the first week laying the groundwork for change by assessing current factors and building relationships with her team, which comprises five administrators. Presently, they seem to like Rachel. Rachel knows, though, that once she starts to push for change and efficiency, fears could multiply about job security and potential redundancies.

Privately, Rachel has scoped out the reasons for the team's inefficiencies. She has noted the following:

- Each of the five administrators views the role as synonymous with being the personal secretary to one of the surveyors. As such, they do not share out the workload. Cheryl only types Robert's building survey. Victoria only types reports for another surveyor; and so on.

- The administrators type building survey reports into Microsoft Word from audio dictations given by the surveyors.

- Some of the older surveyors are reluctant to experiment with technological solutions to speed up the process. For instance, one insists that draft reports (which run to 10,000 words) are printed for him to proofread and edit by hand, before then being re-typed into the computer, approved, and emailed out to clients.

- The administrators enjoy typing. They all trained as audio typists and they do not like to use predictive text, even though it would greatly speed up the process.

- The company does not track the administrators' time. So, there is limited understanding of the cost to the business of these inefficient approaches.

Before we progress to Part II, you should complete the activity overleaf.

- Case study activity: Using a blue pen, underline the words or phrases that describe the problem.

old-fashioned   *unproductive*

slow   *galvanize*   *streamline*

collaborate   *bespoke*

understanding   *upskill*

redundancies   *fear*   *reluctance*

ignorance skills gap   *lack of*

awareness   *measuring*

manual   *analogue*

digital

pressure   *costly*

experimentation

design   *scope*   *reassess*

review

times have changed   *look to the future*

opportunities

2.   Look again at the list above. Underline the words or phrases that offer up solutions.

Part II

To describe the problem, Rachel could speak her mind. She could say to Robert or to her team of administrators:

"We are under a lot of <u>pressure</u>. I have noticed that manual typing is slow and <u>unproductive</u>. Typing from audio dictations is <u>old-fashioned</u> and there should not be such a <u>reluctance</u> to try <u>digital</u> alternatives. I think it comes from a <u>lack of awareness</u> and <u>a skills gap</u>. It is costly. We need to <u>streamline</u> things around here."

Go back to the previous page. For each word you underlined in blue that features in Rachel's speech above, give yourself a point. Hopefully, you score at least five points. If you underlined the word "ignorance" in blue, however, deduct three points. Great managers never describe their team or company as ignorant—not even to themselves.

Next, read Rachel's second speech below. Count how many words match those you underlined in black. Again, each correct word scores you one point. Hopefully, you score at least five points.

"Measuring the time we take on building survey reports will increase our understanding of how to galvanize the process. After that review, we will reassess and collaborate. There are opportunities to upskill and design bespoke solutions."

- Self-assessment

16-17 points. Well done. You are excellently versed in creating solutions with the right words and strategies. You are a sensitive and skilled communicator, who absorbed the lessons from Chapter Two on communicating for greatness. You are well on your way to becoming a great new manager.

10-15 points. Good. You have adequately grasped the distinction between problems and solutions. You understand that great managers remain aware of how they frame issues and communicate about them to their team members and their own managers. That is great.

0-9 points. Some degree of review is required.

If you found it relatively difficult to separate out the language of problems from the language of solutions in the case study activity, you could return to Chapter Two and review the section about problem-solving systems ("solutions systems"). If you scored fewer than five points, you should re-read the fundamentals of communicating for greatness.

- Summary

As a great manager, Rachel avoids describing the problem altogether.

Instead, having carefully considered the factors, Rachel presents her own manager and the people she manages with *productive ideas for positive change.*

Merely by using the right words and choosing the right strategies, Rachel bypasses the problem completely.

Rather, she gets straight to work on creating the solution.

Most importantly, she communicates this in a great way to the people around her.

Chapter Four: Review

1) List five ways to manage your manager:

a. _____

b. _____

c. _____

d. _____

e. _____

2) Summarize what you have learned about *solutions* using no more than twenty words:

_____

_____

_____

_____

_____

_____

Chapter 5: Hiring the Right People

One of the most exciting developments in your new working life is the ability to create your team: not just in the sense of building values, a culture, and dynamics, as we have discussed, but actually hiring the right people for the job, for the group, for the company, and for the future.

Odds are, if you are a new manager then your experience of interviewing and hiring will be limited. It might surprise you to know how hard it can be to enrich your team with people who embody the right talents, skills, personalities, and potentials. It is a cliche, but while hiring these people can be easy, keeping them is far less so. A great manager knows who will stay and how long for, on a balance of probabilities. Great managers hire people with varied strengths for varied roles, resulting in a varied team. They spot opportunities for individual and collective betterment and benefit.

In this way, they ensure the creation of a truly great workforce.

In the section below, we break down the interview process to teach you how to get hiring right the first time and every time. We explore how to optimize your human resources by seeking out diversity and different strengths, all across the board. We give specific examples of what to spot in your potential hires and current team members, so that you can generate a great team for your company.

Getting hiring right: the interview process

Interviews are time-consuming. As a new manager who aspires to greatness, you need to view your time as a valuable resource. Hence, it is important to make sure you do not waste time interviewing candidates who are not serious, not sufficiently skilled, or simply not cut out for the job.

While nobody has a sixth sense, there are plenty of obvious qualities in a good application. In "What to spot", we run through the things to look out for when interviewing candidates. However, you should look for all of those things when screening applications too.

The easiest way to ensure interviews are a smooth, efficient use of your time is to have excellent systems for selecting candidates and for the interview process itself.

When it comes to screening applications, ensure that every application is on file in the same place. This could be as simple as a folder in your inbox. If you have good organizational systems—which you should have, seeing as you have read Chapter Two all the applications will be in one place, ready for your review.

Prior to screening, list three non-negotiables for your new hire. Then, discard any applications that fail to meet these essential criteria. Next, list three key desirable qualities or skills for the role. Continue by discarding applications that do not evidence these. Finally, rank the remaining applications. Invite five candidates to interview. If you have no applications, or not enough applications, you may want to reconsider the initial advert and how it was distributed.

For the interview stage, use a clear criteria to assess your candidates. This could be a company-wide policy, or else a criteria of your own design if no such policy exists. You could use "What to spot" to inform this criteria. After the interviews, assess whether your ranking is borne out by your assessment of the candidates in person; often, it will not be and a new ranking must be drawn. Finally, offer your top candidate the job. If the candidate declines, continue by working your way down the list.

Interviews should take place within the same day and should not last longer than half an hour. Far more complex recruitment policies and interview day structures exist in many large companies and public organizations. They are outside the scope of this section. If your company has a structure for interviews, you must use it.

What to spot

Cookie-cutter approaches are great when you want to make cookies. However, a whole bunch of cookies does not make for a healthy diet. In the same way, cookie-cutter hiring approaches do not create a healthy, balanced team.

In the list below, you will find eight qualities great managers spot in their potential hires (and current team members). By spotting these qualities, and valuing them, great managers ensure they create a well-rounded, varied, diverse team to cover all bases and meet all requirements:

1.   *Openness.* A potential employee who presents as open will be open to change, training, learning, and management.

2.   *Genuine enthusiasm.* Nobody wants a curmudgeon in their team. Happy employees enjoy their work. In turn, they work better and enjoy greater success for themselves and their company. While an over-eager potential hire can fizzle out

when the pedal meets the metal, genuine enthusiasm for a role is something to spot and prize in candidates.

3. *Mix of skills.* Do not misunderstand me here: sometimes you need a specialist. Brain surgeons are not better brain surgeons by virtue of possessing additional knowledge about bookkeeping, for example. However, in many fields and sectors a mix of skills is something to spot—especially in younger hires. So-called "digital natives" often come with a range of abilities that previous generations find harder to acquire. What is more, the rise of the "side hustle" means that your new junior software developer could have blogging experience, too. If you do not ask, you will not be able to gauge what your hires could offer your team beyond the bounds of the job description.

4. *Punctuality.* This old cherry is one to savor. App-based communications and social media have created a widespread culture of casualness and deferred arrangements, whereby appointments are flexible and capable of being rearranged at a moment's notice. As a result, younger hires tend to struggle with punctuality more often than their

seniors. It is a generalization, but it has some truth. Any candidate who cannot be punctual for an interview is one to avoid.

5.   *Courtesy.* In your potential employees, you should look for the hallmarks of courtesy rather than mere manners. This is because "good manners" are culturally constructed and constantly changing. To illustrate this, look no further than the handshake before versus during the Covid-19 pandemic. Courtesy, on the other hand, is eternal.

6.   *Aspiration.* Aspiration is not the same as ambition, which has connotations of material success. Wanting to be a great homemaker, loyal family member, good employee, or moderately prosperous citizen who can keep a roof over their head and bread on the table, are not ambitions. Instead, they are valuable, respectable, laudable aspirations. If you ask your potential hire why they want to work for your company, you will quickly gauge whether they have aspirations. If they do not know why they want the job, it is likely that they lack the necessary awareness to be a great addition to your team.

7.   *Honesty*. Asking your potential hire why they want to work for your company is a great way to assess their honesty, too.

8.   *Collaboration*. There is a reason why interviewers typically ask candidates to describe a time when they worked well in a team setting: potential hires who are merely out for number one have no place in your team. It helps to pay attention to whether the interviewee is using terms like "we", "with", and "together", rather than "I" (which can denote: "me, me, me"). You want employees who collaborate.

On that note, it is helpful to listen out for, or indeed use, a selection of other words that begin with "co-". In addition to "collaboration", try: co-operation, coordination, co-creation, combination, concur, concerted effort, collegiality... Once you have spotted it, it is hard to unsee.

Diverse roles and differing strengths

The word "diversity" is used a lot nowadays. Some people like the word, some people do not.

Diversity is the same as not filling up on cookies. As we have seen, a cookie-cutter team is not healthy or balanced. The same is true for a team that lacks variety.

Diversity can refer to many aspects of a person: age, size, gender, ethnicity, religion, education, national origin, neurological functioning, and physical ablement, are some examples. People are all different and all unique. Likewise, they have different and diverse strengths. As a great new manager, it is your job to cultivate a varied team for the success of everyone in your company.

In the context of your working life as a new manager, diversity also denotes the diverse roles performed by the people in your team.

In other words, diversity exists along two axes. You could plot the strengths and unique qualities of the people in your team along one axis, and the diverse functions they play along the other. Diversity exists everywhere.

As a final note, before we progress to the review section, many companies designate diversity and inclusion officers. If your company does not have one, you could find out why. If there is a need for greater education about diversity, begin by educating yourself. When it comes to telling your team what you know about diversity, you can always start with cookies.

Chapter Five: Review

1.   Summarize the three stages of the pre-screening process for applications:

a.   _____*[List three essential criteria. Discard applications that fail to meet these.]*

b.   _____*[List three desirable qualities or skills. Discard applications that fail to meet these]*.

c.   _____*[Rank the remaining candidates prior to interview]*

2.   What should you do after the interviews are complete?

-       _____*[Review the initial rankings]*

-       _____*[Re-rank candidates based on what you know now]*

-       _____*[Offer the job to the top candidate]*

3. From memory, recall five qualities to spot in potential hires:

_____

_____

_____

[*Any five from: honesty, openness, punctuality, a mix of skills, collaboration, aspiration, courtesy, and genuine enthusiasm*]

4. Now, list five qualities that you deem important in new team members:

_____

_____

_____

5.   In your own words, explain what diversity means to you. Aim to list four or five key facets.

_____

_____

_____

Chapter 6: Making Meetings Manageable

The good old-fashioned "boring meeting" had a makeover in 2020, swiftly morphing into its uglier, tougher, and considerably more challenging alter ego: the Zoom meeting. There are no two ways about it. Meetings were boring long before Covid-19, but they became even more boring during the lockdowns. Since then, the pandemic and its repercussions have changed the face of meetings forever.

For many people, working life under Covid-19 was transformed into a seemingly non-stop stream of remote video calls in March 2020. The reprieves were few and far between. The learning curve was steep for us all, yet ultimately it brought some positives. Having worked through 2020—and suffered through its inexorable online interactions—we view meetings, and the value of our time, differently than before.

As a great first-time or new manager, you will show your team that you understand the importance of their time. You are not going to waste anyone's time with pointless, drawn-out meetings. Rather, you will use strategies and tools to make meetings manageable for your team. What is more, in doing so you will free up your own time. This will empower you to focus on the real work at hand and to achieve more as a manager, all across the board.

However, you should make no mistake: it is not easy to get meetings right. Creating a great first interaction with your new team is hard enough. To illustrate this, just think about everything we covered in Chapter Two about *communicating for greatness*. Getting meetings right—for you, for the company, and for the people you manage—is hard to do one time, let alone every time. Therefore, it is going to take careful consideration on your part of some fundamental rules. Luckily, the section below sets out the principles of manageable meetings clearly.

Meeting the challenge: from mediocre to memorable

By following these tenets, you and your team will maximize your time, efficiency, and productivity. Many of the tips below are memorable. Their usage in a work environment will surprise some of your team members, re-energizing them and their attitude to meetings.

As a result, far from dreading the mediocre meetings of yesteryear, your team will recognize their power to drive progress, enrich working culture, overcome adversity, and facilitate great communication.

Balance leading with participating.

Silence is your ally—especially in meetings.

You should never forget the fact that, in your role as a manager, you are viewed as an authority. Oftentimes, new managers forget this simple reality. Trust me: your mere presence is more than enough to communicate your authority to your team members.

In the light of this, you must bear in mind that you do not need to be speaking in order to lead a meeting. Saying less does not equate to leading less. In fact, great managers tend to use fewer words. By sharing the oxygen with others, everyone breathes easier.

Thus, during meetings you should aim to speak for no more than ten percent of the time available to you. If you aim for that, you will likely hit twenty percent in reality—and that is just fine.

Great managers are aware that meetings are not a forum for them to blather on. Announcements intended for the whole team can easily be communicated over email, if not briefly at the beginning or end of the gathering. Instead, great managers rightfully view meetings as a means of creating solutions and building a team culture.

- *Never use the m-word.*

Back in Chapter Four, we learned how great managers refuse to use the word "problem". In the same vein, you should never let your team know that a meeting is a meeting.

As we have discussed, meetings are not popularly viewed as pleasant, or even tolerable, ways to spend time at work. Everybody is sick to the back teeth of meetings.

Because of this, it is a good idea to reframe a "meeting" as something with altogether fewer teeth—something softer.

You can defang the prospect of a meeting by employing one of the cuddlier, more casual words commonly used to this end. Such terms include: catch ups, huddles, chats, get-togethers, working lunches, pre-sprints, focus panels, and discussion groups. Great managers, however, come up with their own bespoke phrases, rejecting buzzwords. Finding your own substitutes for the m-word will suit your individual context better, helping to create a strong team identity.

- *Consider the realities of time and space.*

First, time. Only bad managers opt for overlong, tedious meetings that slip from minutes into hours. What is more, although good managers are aware that they should keep it brief, often they fall prey to overestimating the time available and underestimating the time it takes to explore an issue properly. To combat this, aim to discuss no more than three matters in your meeting. This allows plenty of space for others to chip in and derail your agenda, which is an inevitable part of human interaction at work and beyond it.

Regular, short meetings are infinitely preferably to infrequent, longer ones.

Second, space. Think about where your meeting is to be held. Are the facilities adequate, comfortable, pleasant, or inspiring? Will coffee or refreshments be provided? Is the room hot, cold, or ambient, noisy, quiet, or just right? It might sound like the stuff of Goldilocks, but great managers consider where their team members are meeting. Since great managers value the people they manage, they understand how important this is to get right.

A perfect meeting room is great. Yet actually, varying the location of your team meetings can really help to keep things fresh.

You could consider the following venues and strategies.

-    Meeting at a different team member's desk—perhaps someone whose contribution you wish to highlight on that occasion

-    Walking meetings: take your team on a brief trip around the workplace or its vicinity, but secretly hold a meeting. They will enjoy the tour so much that many will fail to notice that it was just a pretext for another team meeting.

- Meeting in a different location in the office each time: around the water-cooler, in the breakout room, at your desk, at your boss's desk, in the fanciest meeting room available... anywhere, as long as it is different

-    Standing up. Why not ban everybody from sitting down (health issues excepted, naturally) for

the next six meetings? It keeps a team on its toes—
and their manager, too!

- *Keep it simple, keep it small.*

Certain meetings scale very poorly. One example is
product reviews, which rapidly descend into chaos
and abstraction when opened up to too many
invitees.

Effective meetings are not just short. They are not
just about sharing oxygen, ideas, and solutions.
Great managers keep their meetings simple and
small, for the good of their team and of all.

Chapter Six: Review

1. List five tips you will consider using to improve your meetings with your team this month.

_____

_____

_____

_____

_____

2. Place the following statements on the line diagram.

Write the letters only.

Disagree———————————————————————Agree

a. *I am confident when leading a meeting*

b. *I find that I get easily bored at times when I am not speaking*

c. *I expect all my team members to participate in meetings*

d. *Remote meetings are never as good as in-person alternatives*

e. *Agendas are necessary for successful meetings*

f. *The time and space chosen for the meeting contributes to its success (or failure)*

g. *Meetings should achieve outcomes*

h. *Meetings are an opportunity to air concerns*

i. *Meetings help to build team culture*

j. *Taking minutes helps to ensure that meetings are impactful*

3. Use the space below to plan your next team meeting.

You may wish to take a photocopy of the blank meeting template first, so that you can reuse it to plan future meetings too.

Date_____

Planned start time_____

Planned finish time_____

Location_____

Number/names of attendees:

Described to my team not as a *meeting* but as a...

Purpose of meeting:

First point of order:

- _____

- _____

- _____

Second point of order:

- _____

- _____

- _____

Final point of order:

- _____

- _____

- _____

Summary of what I want my team to take away:

4.   After filling out your meeting template, and leading the meeting, you should make sure to record any reflections using a suitable system.

Chapter 7: Empowering Your Team with Feedback

Once upon a time, managers were taught to deliver good news, bad news, and good news again, when giving feedback to their team members.

Pardon my French, but this unpleasant strategy was known as a "sh*t sandwich". Moreover, it was every bit as nasty as it sounds.

Great managers do not view the feedback process as an opportunity to smuggle cold, hard facts under the radar. They do not need to hide the truth. It is easy to see why you should never couch bad news in the language of good. Disguising harsh truths is dishonest. In terms of its effects, the "shi*t sandwich" approach benefits nobody. Unless a problem is addressed— ideally by creating a solution, as we explored in Chapter Four—it will persist. It will never be addressed if it is sandwiched between platitudes and misrepresented as merely an unusual, unpalatable filling.

Great managers do not shy away from communicating unpleasant or difficult realities to the people whom they manage. Rather, they use everything they know about *communicating for greatness* to rise to this challenge.

What is more, they know how to create solutions, rather than centering on problems, as we saw in Chapter Four.

So, as a great new manager you will need to empower your team with valuable, truthful feedback—both good and bad.

In the following two sections, we will first look at how great managers *identify the good* and then *work towards betterment*. Afterwards, we study how such managers *accept the bad* and wield valuable feedback to *ameliorate—at all times*.

Identifying the good

Relatively speaking, it is easy to identify the good. At least, with you in charge, there ought to be plenty of positives to spot, praise, and encourage in your team members.

Where an employee is performing exceedingly poorly, we are tipping away from the topic of feedback towards the domain of dealing with difficulty and firing weak hires.

For now, you should be reassured that there will almost always be good things to identify in your team members when giving them feedback. Even *the good* is not a tangible output, it is worth consulting the list of *What to spot* in Chapter Five. Although this is addressed in the section on desirable traits to look out for in potential new team members, it applies to your current team members too. Perhaps the employee in question has displayed an aspect of these laudable qualities, even if they have not produced a quantifiable good.

Working towards betterment

Once you have started out by *identifying the good*, working towards the better becomes so much easier, both for you and for your team members. Having set out to recognize their strengths—and having spotted *something*, at least, that your team member is doing well—they are already bound to feel encouraged. That is a great foundation to build on. Needless to say, because you are a master communicator you will have made sure to frame your team member's successes as something that belongs *solely to them*—even if it was actually a joint effort. Success should always be phrased as being something that *your team members own*, all by themselves. Meanwhile, any areas for development should always be articulated as being *your shared responsibility,* since great managers do not shy away from taking ownership of their team members: warts and all.

Targets, too, are better framed as a shared effort. Simply by using phrases like: *"let's work towards..."*; *"how about we now focus on..."*; or *"a good new target for us would be..."*, your team member will feel supported in their areas for development.

Accepting the bad

According to the traditional view of the workplace, an excellent employee is flawless. A good employee avoids errors at all costs and is cautious, methodical, and diligent. But in actuality, mistakes are made by even the most careful and attentive workers. In this world, nobody is flawless. Even excellent managers err. And that isn't always a terrible thing.

It is easy to chastise and criticize when a mistake is made, but this is not what a competent manager does. A great manager investigates the cause of a mistake rather than blaming the person who started the fire. You should be aware that innovation necessitates bold decision-making and taking risks. When you take risks, mistakes and complete failures occur from time to time. Instead of chastising the individual who started the fire as the lava approaches the coast, your first duty is to intervene and try to remedy the situation. In order to find out why, ask probing inquiries. Try asking questions such as, "*What was running through your mind?*" *What outcome did you anticipate?* The majority of the time, the error stems from good intentions. Ask yourself, "Could I have stated things better?" Where did I go wrong in my expectations setting?

As a manager, you shouldn't bestow the impossible-to-maintain mantle of perfection on your top people. You are responsible for the individuals you lead. And sometimes that involves accepting responsibility for the mistakes of others. It is your responsibility to bear the majority of the blow if you are in the driver's seat, even if the person in the backseat triggered the incident. This will help instill loyalty in your staff. They are considerably more likely to strive hard not to let you down again.

Ameliorating—at all times

Mistakes are rarely the result of a single cause, and people are not always to blame. After accepting and identifying the root cause of a mistake, take some time to reflect on all you've heard and determine what, if anything, you may have done to enhance company operations. Should you, for example, hold a specific training session for employees or supplement verbal communication with a written protocol manual?

Mistakes are an opportunity for you to learn as well. Making minor modifications can result in significant benefits. You can start investing time and energy in individual or team coaching, and you could even appoint another employee to serve as a mentor to whom an error-prone employee can turn if they have questions.

Communicate to your team that you have a team culture that welcomes inquiry, accepts mistakes, and rewards solutions. Focus on solving the problem and preventing it from happening again, rather than assigning blame. consider ways to avoid future blunders, While there is no way to avoid mistakes forever, you can take actionable steps to reduce the likelihood of them happening in the future. Take some time to step back and examine the system, process, structure, and so on that may have contributed to the mistake. Perhaps such errors could be avoided with greater training, communication, and/or processes.

In the next chapter, training methods will be discussed extensively, as it is your biggest step towards ameliorating.

Chapter Seven: Review

What do you need to empower your team with?

_____

_____

List five positives to spots in your team members

_____

_____

Write 2 new supportive phrases you intend to use in future

_____

_____

List off hand 3 questions you should ask yourself when a team member makes a mistake

_____

_____

Chapter 8: Training the People You Manage for Greatness

Congratulations: you have reached the halfway point of this book. That means you are well on your way to becoming a great new or first-time manager: the kind who gets it right.

Furthermore, if you have been following this book to the letter (and if you have not, then I suggest you take the opportunity now to return to any sections you cannot recall, or else risk losing the valuable investment you have made in your own success), you will understand the importance of training your team. After all, great managers want greatness for everybody, not just themselves.

Yet when it comes to the nitty gritty ins and outs of training and professional development, you might need some practical assistance. With the abundance of options out there, even great managers will experience a moment of bafflement the first time they sit down to look for solutions to their team's training requirements.

In this chapter, we will cover the topic comprehensively to dispel ambiguities and arm you with strategies. We will look first at how to assess skills gaps, before exploring training timescales, structures, and means of delivery. We will compare the benefits and demerits of internal and external training options and look at that behemoth of the training landscape: opting to train your team yourself. Finally, we will summarize what you as a manager can do to create a culture of continuous learning, progress, and success for your team—and yourself.

Training for greatness

As we have discussed in the previous chapter, ameliorating basically involves making good what was bad. When team members make mistakes, it is up to you to evaluate the situation, access their needs and provide solutions. In this case, our problem is skills and our solution is training. The tight relationship between you and your team extends to training as well, given that you are familiar with the skill your company needs, and, most crucially, your team.

Even if your firm has a strong learning culture, it is critical to communicate to your staff that training and development is a key priority. You must convince them of the importance of employee development activities and how such initiatives will benefit them and the organization in the long run. Whether they are cross-training to understand multiple roles or moving into new positions, team members can prepare for additional responsibilities. Training programs can help your staff stay up to date on changes in their industry, such as changes in ethics, safety, or quality standards. Using these new tools and techniques in their day-to-day duties can result in greater outcomes for your team and company.

However, to train your team for success, you must not only know how to train them but also what you should teach them.

As promised, the next section will provide you with all you need to access the needs of your team members.

Skill Gaps

One of the most efficient ways to determine training needs of your team is by analyzing skill gaps. A skills gap analysis will help you identify the talents your team presently possesses and the skills they will require in the future.

You must get it right if you want to properly teach your staff, Otherwise, you might just be on the verge of wasting time and money.

The question is, how do you get it right?

Determine your team's objectives.

Prior to doing anything at all, it's critical to define the team's objectives. It's important to be clear about what you want from your team. Identify your objectives to decide the responsibilities that will be required both now and in the future. For instance, as part of a larger initiative to modernize customer relationship management generally, you could discover that customer support activity that is presently performed by phone will be undertaken online. People who work the phone and email will thus need to learn how to handle chat, video conferencing, and other social channels.

Create a list of these objectives to act as a reminder.

Make a list of the qualifications needed for each position.

For assistance in creating a list of the essential skills necessary for certain tasks, consult a variety of sources. Some recruiting companies specialize in conducting cross-organizational comparison studies to create skill inventories. Individual countries also provide official occupational categories that detail the skills required for each. Additionally, if you wish to complete the task internally, you may gather the skills list using job ads from professional websites, such as LinkedIn. Once you receive the list of qualifications needed for a certain position, you must prioritize them in one of two ways:

- Skill type
- Degree of competence

By doing this, each position will become clearer and easier to manage.

Draw up a list of the abilities your staff members already possess.

It's time to find out where your team stands right now. This is a crucial indicator of skill gaps, thus you must be attentive when performing it. When attempting to pinpoint workplace skill shortages, it is advisable to concentrate on data collection approaches. Data, after all, reinforces analytical findings and, in the end, correctly validates and identifies skill shortages.

There are several ways you may evaluate your staff. However, I advise using at least three alternative approaches. Diverse ways will not only provide you with different viewpoints on the problem, but they will also give you additional knowledge about the actual problems and their underlying causes.

Best techniques

- Employee evaluation

And how do you evaluate your staff? That's simple: examinations and quizzes are typical methods, but there are also other approaches like practical evaluations or role-playing exercises. One important thing to remember is to base the evaluations on realistic work situations so you can spot skill gaps and training requirements for what they are.

- Conduct comprehensive reviews.

Feedback is a useful tool for identifying skill deficiencies. The 360-degree review is a sort of performance evaluation that collects information based on feedback from peers and direct reports about an employee's performance. Clients, consumers, and suppliers are occasionally included in this kind of study.

- Observation.

Observation, or paying attention to the situation during regular business activities in the workplace, is a particularly efficient method of determining skill gaps. Usually, as a diligent manager who has mastered the techniques in this book to interact with and communicate with their team, this should be exceptionally simple for you; if not, you might want to return to chapter 2 and read in-depth about being a good manager to your team.

Observe by watching how each person functions throughout the day to gain important insights into what is working and what isn't. Direct observations may provide you with a more thorough understanding of employee performance and skill gaps, as well as assist you to pinpoint exactly where things are going wrong.

- Benchmarking

There are two approaches to this:

Determine which employees have demonstrated excellent talents by comparing them to other top performers in similar roles.

Using the company's standards to assess skill level is an alternative strategy; to do this properly, you might also refer to the job description of the person.

- Utilize specialized software to assess staff.

Performance evaluation software is widely accessible on the market. The only thing you need to worry about is selecting the software for your team.

Given that every person is different, It might be difficult to select software that matches your needs.

Taking a look at employee performance assessment samples can help you decide which aspects are most essential to you to choose the best appraisal software for your employee reviews.

Conduct a skill-gap analysis.

It's time to get down to business and compare the capabilities your workers now have to the skills you require from them. The skills gap you'll be bridging is the disparity between those two components.

Make an individual skills spreadsheet for each person based on the data you gathered in the earlier phases.

There's a format that you can practice with in the review session .

Bridging The Gap

It's time to close the gap between what your team needs and what they already have once you've evaluated them and determined their strengths and shortcomings.

Effective training is the greatest strategy for dealing with this. The section below provides a step-by-step explanation of how to conduct training sessions, including information on session organization, training techniques, and training durations.

Your Very First Training Plan

Now that you already know what skills are lacking in your team, and what skills are abundant. It is time to build up on the existing skills or learn new ones entirely to increase the overall productivity of your team.

You should go by these instructions in order to make your first staff training session a success.

Setting objectives for the training program.

- Setting goals is the first step to well-targeted and successful training. Clear training attempts to do more than just answer the audience's question "What's in it for me?" They connect the training to the business' goals and measurable outcomes.

Start by considering what you hope to achieve through staff training initiatives and how doing so will advance your company's objectives. Define your training objectives using the information you obtained during your skill gap study.

- Once you have determined your training objectives, it is time to write them down. These will serve as both the foundation for your training program and your strongest promotional material.

- Make the training program's goal clear. What do you want to achieve from this training course? Enhance worker performance? Fill a knowledge void? Whatever the situation, you need to make sure that the training's goal is obvious.

- Keep in mind that training regimens are not created by magic. There is always a reason why training is necessary, and the skill gap analysis you completed earlier will make it simpler for you to create and write training objectives.

Define the desired training results.

The success (or failure) of your training approach is determined by the results since you will judge training based on whether or not your teams have attained these goals.

Make sure you are explicit and allow no room for debate when describing the anticipated training outcomes. Be careful not to use imprecise phrases like "understand," "realize," and "learn." Instead, use verbs like "make," "demonstrate," and "compute" that convey actual, visible action.

Your training objectives should be listed using the SMART approach, which may be encapsulated in five letters (specific, measurable, attainable, relevant, and time-bound)

For example;

NOT SMART;

Readers will understand how to define training results

SMART;

At the end of this section(time bound, attainable), managers who read this book will be able to define the desired results(specific, measurable) for their next training session(relevant)

NOT SMART;

participants will understand the use of social media

SMART;

After 1 week of training (time bound, attainable) the PR team will be able to utilize social media platforms(specific,measurable) to make promotion easier and to reach a wider audience(relevant)

Because producing business results is the primary objective of training. Make sure that learning outcomes are in line with organizational objectives.

So, unless staff training objectives are based on business criteria, training will be a waste of time and money

Select the Training Method that Best Suits Your Goals and Spending plan

The next phase in the staff training strategy is to select training techniques that are appropriate for your team members.

To identify the best employee training approach for your training program, you must first analyze your employees' learning styles.

Depending on your objectives and budget, you have two options for your training program: either train in-house by employing team members with higher abilities as trainers (internal) or engage an outside consultant "trainers" or third party to run your programs (external).

We'll talk about the two training techniques you may use, but you should pick the one that you and your team feel work best for you.

Before you choose a training program, take into account the available training budget and the results you hope to achieve from the complete training process.

Other significant aspects to consider when selecting a training technique include training objectives, timeline/duration of training sessions, organizational culture, team size, remote or office-based setting, and so on.

Internal training

Sessions for internal training are led by an employee of your business. This may be a more senior employee with greater experience - it all depends on the aim of the session and who the ideal person for the job is.

This training program may be delivered in a variety of ways, including roleplaying, group activities, and on-the-job training.

The team-based interactions fostered by internal training enable the less seasoned personnel to advance professionally by encouraging knowledge acquisition and transfer. When choosing a coach for a learner, you should take into account a few criteria; specifically, you should consider:

Experience.

The experience gaps between the coach and the trainee shouldn't be excessively wide or narrow. The trainees must be capable of growth and challenge without being overburdened.

Expectations.

Both sides must be aware of what to anticipate from the partnership.

Compatibility.

The connection is frequently considerably more successful when trainers and trainees communicate in ways that are comparable to one another. Consider using evaluation to pair together individuals with similar personalities.

Pros

Setting up internal training sessions is simple since you already have everyone and everything you require. As a result, planning is also simpler and less expensive.

An experienced team member mentoring less experienced team members can aid in the development of connections and a team spirit. Even the trainer could pick up some new skills from the less experienced team members.

Internal training sessions do not merely educate new employees or provide team members with a refresher. Additionally, they may assist the tutor in filling in any knowledge gaps and reinforcing what they already know.

Cons

The more time we spend with a certain team or person inside an organization, the simpler it is to fall victim to groupthink.

Employees are more likely to become lonely and mired in their routines, both of which can be harmful over time.

Every sector of the economy is changing quickly in the era of technology. Teams or businesses who operate in isolation run the danger of lagging behind their rivals and using antiquated methods that might harm their reputation and bottom line.

External training

External training is provided by specialists or personalities from outside your organization.

They might be someone with whom your firm already has a connection, such as a supplier, who has been brought in to provide further information on a product or feature, or they could be an industry expert who can discuss the newest trends to assist teams to keep ahead of the competition.

When using this form of training, it must allocate your staff to certain training programs. Along with fundamental business skills and soft skill training, these courses should cover job-specific competencies.

This training approach can take a range of forms, including online video courses, which can be pre-made films on popular subjects or videos that are specially created.

Pros

External training sessions dispel groupthink and provide a new perspective on the way things are done. This might significantly change how things are done going forward . It's like giving someone new eyes; they will undoubtedly see differently. They may see more clearly or less clearly.

Teams can learn from subject matter experts in the business through external training events. Your team will be able to break out of their routine and see things from a fresh perspective by introducing trainers with other perspectives.

The most effective of these training courses typically employ blended learning, which combines both sessions led by instructors and digital/online media. Digital courses may free up teachers' time when used in a blended learning strategy, enabling them to use class time for more beneficial activities like group discussions, or question and answer sessions.

Learning from a person whose job is to keep up with industry developments, also helps to prospect the knowledge of your staff. The tutors' knowledge from dealing with dozens or hundreds of businesses will enable them to recognize certain patterns that are shared throughout training sessions.

Cons

Although outside training might give your employees new insights from knowledgeable instructors, they are more costly than in-house training. If your budget cannot handle this, you might want to think about taking the other route.

The planning process could also take longer. Choosing professionals might be challenging because the finest individuals are usually quite busy.

Online classes and courses frequently have a certain number of slots available or are only accessible at particular times of the year. If you choose online training, it could be challenging to find courses that are available when you need them for your staff to participate.

Choose training technology

To build and assign training courses to employees, measure progress, and track completion rates, you may focus on employee training software like video learning methods, corporate learning management systems, etc. Because they use a variety of interactive learning techniques, these technologies will assist you in standardizing the employee training process throughout the team.

Assemble a group to provide interesting and useful training materials. The team may originate from within the organization in the case of internal training or from a third-party supplier in the case of external training. It may contain:

- a project director
- educational architects
- graphic designers
- instructors for in-person or online classes
- professionals in their areas (SMEs)

This phase will be taken care of by the third-party supplier if you are working with them. They will arrive at a development plan. You'll receive a timetable from them outlining the timing of each stage's completion.

Determine effectiveness

We want to make sure that our training objectives are met after we're done. You can determine if your training programs are effective by tracking improvements in employee overall performance.

Ask the employees:

What new information, such as a job, tool, or talent, did you learn from the program?

How do you intend to apply your freshly learned knowledge?

What about the process did you like, and what might we have improved upon (such as the topic, approach, teacher, or content)?

The methods you used to gather data on skill gaps may also be used to evaluate the effectiveness of your team's training programs.

Feedback.

Collect post-training employee feedback through interviews or anonymous online surveys to determine whether the training program helped employees learn new skills or improve their existing ones.

Employee assessment.

After the course, provide tests or quizzes to see how well the participants understood what they have been taught

Observation.

Keep an eye on your staff to see whether they are applying the new knowledge to their usual work.

Analytical tools.

The training program's data analytics dashboard may be used to assess how workers are reacting to the training.

Productivity.

After a month or a quarter, evaluate the effects of your training to determine whether there have been any changes in sales, costs, employee production, etc.

Smaller, more frequent training sessions are more effective than larger, irregular instructional blips. Try to establish a consistent learning and development culture at your workplace to encourage your team to pursue personal and professional growth.

Chapter Eight: Review

List the 5 stages of skill gap analysis

_____

_____

_____

_____

_____

What 3 approaches do you intend to use for gathering data on skills possessed by your team members?

_____

_____

_____

Why did you choose those approaches?

_____

_____

_____

What 5 goals do you want to achieve with your next employee training?

_____

_____

_____

_____

_____

Write your those same goals using the SMART format

_____

_____

_____

_____

_____

There are 2 training methods, which one do you think suits your team best?

_____

Why? (There's no limit to your number of whys)

_____

_____

_____

Write a structured plan for training a particular employee using this template

Name:(*Name of employee*)

Date: (*dd,mm,yy*)

Current role:

Learning gap:

Training goals:

Learning outcomes:

Type of training:(internal or external)

Additional resources:

Success measures:

Training completed by: (time for completion)

Next meeting:(feedback)

Chapter 9: Creating Your Team Culture

You may have entered your leadership position with a team that has already been formed or, fortunately, are given the chance to form your own group. Whatever the situation, you must create new team cultures across your team.

Every team has a culture, which encapsulates all of the ways in which the team communicates, values, and prioritizes as a unit. You should keep in mind that team culture is a representation of your common beliefs and methods of operation and that it is created by both group and individual activities inside the team.

Good team culture is one in which every member of the group feels valued as an individual and is in alignment with the team's mission, values, attitudes, and methods of operation.

You should not have any trouble creating a positive team culture because you have already acquired the managerial abilities and values that were covered previously in this book. As you already know team members need to be aware of their roles within the group as well as their individual and collective goals. They must understand the motivation for their job and have faith in the team's objectives.

When you implement effective team cultures You'll be able to advance your team and business while also fostering development, happiness, and happiness in the lives of others.

Even though team culture can develop naturally, creating a team culture requires intention, effort, and enthusiasm. Additionally, it calls for particular leadership traits as well as tactical moves that foster an environment conducive to the success of strong teams. The rewards are enormous, but it requires a lot of consciousness, mentoring, nurturing, planning, and modification.

You must establish your culture collectively and agree on what it entails and how you practice it as you develop your team. This might require drafting a statement about your team's culture or a code of behavior, or it could just be trying to improve the ties and mutual understanding of your team.

This chapter will cover the specifics of how strong team cultures are created as well as methods for putting them into practice at work.

Creating a remarkable team culture

One of the finest methods to accomplish tasks in any organization as you already know is through teamwork. An amazing amount of motivation and innovation will be generated when you take a group of individuals with diverse abilities and set them on such a team where they can combine their talents. It doesn't just boost their performance, their loyalty and engagement will be significantly boosted as well.

The most important thing to understand when you begin any sort of initiative for your team is that words do not establish culture; actions do.

Follow these strategic steps to create a solid culture for your team

Strategic steps

1. Establish Your Team's Individual Values and Conduct.

As the team leader, your first step towards creating a good team culture is to what ideals and values you and your team wish to bring into the workplace.

It is always advised to consult with the team before deciding on your values. If your organization has corporate values that you support (even if they aren't being upheld at the present), you can utilize those values as a point of reference and spend your time defining and discussing what they can signify for your team.

Why not assign everyone homework that requires them to consider the desired principles in advance and be ready to talk about how they are significant?

Using sticky notes is a quick and simple approach to finding common topics. Ask everyone to list their ideals for the group (one per sticky note).

After that, arrange the sticky notes into categories.

2. Discuss how to put the values into practice as tangible behaviors

The process of selecting team values is simple; all you have to do is think of a few positive things and choose them. The art of putting these beliefs into actual behaviors, however, might be more difficult.

If, for instance, you have picked empathy as your primary team value, what exactly does it mean?

How can you use it concerning your job?

How do you treat people with compassion, especially your coworkers and vendors?

While it may be simple for you as a manager, you must make sure that your team is equally aware of and capable of interpreting the values which you have chosen together.

Actual clarity is produced when these aspirational principles are put to the test against real-life situations, which aids in problem-solving and decision-making later on.

3. *Create a Basis to Endorse Your Principles*

The ability to reward actions that reflect the team values may be restricted for you as a manager. However, you have some control over what you notice, applaud, and disregard.

Teams with strong team cultures constantly seek out opportunities to honor and acknowledge actions that are consistent with their core principles.

If, for instance, you claim to respect collaboration but choose to ignore it when a team member disrespects his coworkers, your words will be overridden by the effect of your silence.

4. Demand accountability from team members

Great team cultures are characterized by members acting in accordance with the shared values of the group.

When you claim to cherish integrity, you are committing to one another's ability to keep your word. team members should hold each other accountable for honoring agreements in addition to working hard to uphold their collective responsibilities.

Positive team cultures to adopt

Here are some useful positive attributes for you and your team.

Leadership that Pays Attention

Motivating employees to work hard is a key component of creating a great workplace culture.

Encourage your staff, recognize their accomplishments, keep lines of communication open, and foster respect and cooperation among coworkers, all of these will make your team an excellent one.

Make sure that the individuals you choose to join your team represent the principles ingrained in your corporate structure. Try to be as understanding of your staff members' needs as you are able to be by paying attention to what they have to say.

You may show your team members that you appreciate and trust them by listening to their ideas, this might mean implementing a flexible work schedule or incorporating fresh perspectives into your initiatives.

Assistance To All

You won't always run smoothly. The strength of your team will be put to the test during difficult times. When you are winning, everything is simple, but what forms a genuinely positive team culture is how the team handles adversity.

Create a consistently supportive culture, however, Of course, creating this kind of environment requires striking a fine balance. Encourage dependability; as a team, you should be able to rely on your teammates.

Autonomy

Employees enjoy having a sense of trust and independence. In a workplace with an autonomous culture, everyone is encouraged to speak freely, think for themselves, and to make decisions independently.

To establish a pleasant and supportive culture, your team must understand that you believe in them just as much as they do in you

Continuous Innovation

As a manager you should always seek to learn new ways of doing things. This attitude should also be spread across the team. No one progresses by doing the same things the same way. Those that are proactive and inventive like being on the cutting edge of things. Be imaginative at work to create a culture that colleagues adore. Find methods to make your products better, and don't be hesitant to change things up.

Idea Generation and Feedback

People get great job satisfaction working in an environment where their efforts and thoughts have an impact. If you want to create a workplace culture where your colleagues may succeed, then you must provide individuals with a voice. To do this, you can host enjoyable brainstorming sessions and get input from your staff. Implement suggestions by changing processes and allowing for more flexibility. Team members will often remain in the company for longer if you build a great environment where they feel valued.

Praise and appreciation

An important factor in boosting morale and maintaining a happy atmosphere is recognition. When objectives are met and improvements are made, you should express your appreciation. Recognizing great work and collective successes boosts productivity. Team members will be more likely to mimic your conduct if you set the greatest example and consistently give them praise, helping to create a collaborative environment.

Recognize and Reward Contributions

An engaging and stimulating workplace culture recognizes and rewards people for their effort and dedication. Be sure to give your folks rewards for regular attendance, little achievements, and even ordering lunch for the team once every so often. Make sure that yours is a place of work where teamwork is valued and rewarded, and make it apparent that when the team succeeds, everyone on the team succeeds. People will turn up eager to participate when they are confident that both their small and large contributions will be rewarded. The more your team functions like a true team, the more motivated members will be to support your success.

Fun and humor

Make space for humor and enjoyment to create an exciting team culture.
No workplace where assigning blame and negativity is normal, can foster a culture where employees like

going to work and are curious to learn new things. Allowing your staff to relax and enjoy themselves in a respectful manner will inspire them. Good, innocent humor should be cherished, and everyone should be cordial and at ease in one other's company. When employees feel at ease in their workplace, their creativity soars, propelling your team to new heights.

The following chapter will go into great detail on how to bring enjoyment to the workplace; examples and the value of enjoyable activities will be covered.

Chapter Nine: Review

List 3 new values you're bringing into your team

_____

_____

How do you translate each of these values?

_____

_____

List 5 ways you intend to provide for and encourage support in your team

_____

_____

Chapter 10: Spurring Success by Sparking Team Spirit

We have all heard about the dull and boring team events that nobody really wants to attend. From painful paintballing to cliched trust-enhancing activities, building team spirit all too often feels like a chore. Naturally, when that is the case, such activities do nothing for your team's spirit and success.

Yet if you choose to be a little more daring, and tap into people's interests outside of work—which will be easy for you, since you paid close attention to Chapter Two's lessons about *Understanding your team*—you can create unforgettable team building moments that serve your function as a great new manager.

Different ideas, different teams

Not all of the following ideas for unique events and activities will be suitable for your team. After all, your team is unique too.

It would be wise to take time to consider the list in the light of the individuals comprising your team. Then, choose three favorites and aim to trial them over the next four months.

T-shirts

Things will go wrong from time to time. But if you can fix and learn from them, they can be a way to build camaraderie in your team.

Case Study - turning mistakes into humor:

I managed a cross-functional team who was working on the development of an online math learning program. As part of this, we had a large math glossary developed. Each math term had a picture and an explanation of the term under the picture. These terms were created by a separate team in a different country.

But one image got confused along the way, and it was never spotted until our end client (who our company was working for) saw it. It was meant to be a picture of a mathematical tree diagram. But instead, someone had used a picture of a tree! Of course we apologized, fixed it straight away and put in another round of checks to make sure our images were 100% in future.

But a few weeks later when we were celebrating meeting our deadline, I arrived at work with 20 t-shirts with a picture of the unfortunate 'tree' on it. Our team thought it was hilarious and the entire team wore t-shirts all day. It made everyone smile.

So never underestimate the power of a funny t-shirt.

Case study - the weekend away

A weekend away is a fun way to break down barriers and let people get to know each other better. A few years ago I organized a weekend in the country, complete with a day's horse racing for a group of 25 people I worked with.

This was not sponsored by the company - everyone paid for themselves. The country house we stayed in was huge, old and full of character. One lady nearly got stuck in the elevator, in another room the bath wouldn't stop and overflowed by accident, requiring some help from the hotel staff and we were all still up singing along to one of our team who played guitar until 3am in the morning.

The next day, we all went horse racing, and that evening there were some great stories of who had won the most money on the day. That evening again, more music & guitar playing ensued. The entire weekend was a total success, everyone enjoyed it immensely and everyone who missed out wished they had been there.

Case study - The rock band

Outside of work, it's likely people have lots of different & random hobbies. Some of the people I worked with had a music background. One fall it was decided that we would put together a 'work' rock band.

The idea is we would rehearse one evening a week for 2 months, and then perform the best of the 70's and 80's at our Christmas party for 50 minutes, before the DJ appeared. The company we worked for provided some funds to book our recording space each week (it needed to be somewhere sound proofed with an am & drum kit, that a normal band would use to practice in).

Our band name was "The Anticipated Mistakes'. The band consisted of 4 guitars, 1 keyword, 1 bass, 1 drummer, 3 backing singers and 1 soloist. So it was quite a large band.

The band became minor celebrities at work and it was a great conversation point. It created a lot of goodwill between the band members, but also captured the imagination of all staff members!

On the night of our Christmas party performance (we were all dressed as 60's rock stars), we had so many instruments plugged into the hotels power supply, that within the first few seconds of starting playing, we blew the fuse and the room went silent & the lights went out. It was fixed in a few minutes by hotel staff, and we went on to play a legendary set which our entire company adored. The satisfaction, fun & feeling of accomplishment & team building this band generated was incredible.

Build and donate.

This charitable team-building exercise encourages team members to work together and unite them. Team members can build something, give it away to a good cause, then enjoy the benefits as a group

You'll come together in support of a distinct and realistic goal. As you savor the success of a team effort, you'll experience its epicness. As you transfer your contribution, a strong link will form between you.

Everyone can observe the results of their collaboration through this exercise. The finished product will reveal everything, so they won't have to worry about making a sufficient contribution or performing well. This can even be just as simple as a Friday cake sale of homemade cakes.

Play board or team games.

You don't need me to tell you that board games are an excellent way to foster interpersonal relationships, and there are many wonderful, work-friendly alternatives available!

You can introduce games that demand cooperation such as Jenga, Code Names, Pandemic, Apples to Apples, etc. There are other non-tabletop games that don't require much more than a phone or a pen and paper.

Playing games amid work may seem frivolous, but you will be shocked to learn that it really relaxes your team and encourages them to collaborate in novel and imaginative ways.

Chapter Ten: Review

List at least 5 new fun activities you are bringing into your workplace.

_____

_____

_____

_____

_____

Give 2 reasons for choosing each of them.

_____

_____

_____

Chapter 11: Working Effectively, Working Remotely

As you've been reading this book right from the beginning, you've already learned a lot about managing your team well, from successful meetings to strong team values to solid communication, but all of this advice is focused on your physical team. What about those who work remotely?

Being skilled at managing remote workers demands a mental leap; it's a whole different atmosphere, and it could be difficult for some managers. This won't be the case for you, though, as you will receive a detailed explanation and instruction on how to oversee your remote team.

But before that, you might have been wondering, "this whole remote working thing, what makes it better" ? or say an employee comes to you with the request to work remotely, "should you or should you not let them"? Or even, have you been considering working remotely but you don't know if it's the best option? Well after previewing the benefits and the downsides to this concept, you will be able to answer your questions and give your responses right.

Benefits of Remote working

The foundation of remote working is the idea that work doesn't have to be completed in a certain location to be effective. There are several advantages to working remotely, one of which is that it gives employees more freedom because they are not restricted by a certain schedule.

Remote workers may carry out their tasks and achieve their objectives wherever they wish, as opposed to making the daily commute to an office to work from a certain workstation. People have the freedom to plan their days in a way that allows their work and personal life to coexist harmoniously and to the maximum extent possible.

Another benefit of working remotely is that it saves time and money. Employees don't have to wake up earlier than usual, spend more time traveling to and from work, or spend additional money on gas or tickets. They don't have to worry about bad weather, traffic, or potential delays because all they have to do is turn on their computer at the appropriate moment and log in to the system.

Working remotely encourages efficiency and focus. Employees who work from home aren't bothered by office chatter or the constant tapping of keyboards which is a necessary component of an office environment.

They are given all the calm and tranquility they need to focus completely, which results in effective work.

Finally, during job interviews, you may have discovered someone who satisfies all of your requirements and seems ideal for you, but the distance seems insurmountable. Remote working overcomes this and enables an employee to work from any location in the globe. This way, there are more employment options for businesses, and there are more work chances for job seekers.

Disadvantages of Remote Working

As the expression goes, there are two sides to every coin, and while remote working offers advantages, it also has disadvantages. A portion of it being;

Household distractions. Screaming kids, road noise, and housework are just a few of the numerous distractions at home that might prevent a worker from concentrating on their job. It's critical that workers have a designated workplace, access to childcare, and a routine if they plan to continue working from home.

Another difficulty of routinely working from home is the sense of isolation from the team and the overall energy of the office. It is true that working in a calm environment promotes mental clarity and productivity. But after a time, it's easy to miss the excitement of having "things going on," especially with nothing but ideas and the infrequent phone call to interrupt the stillness.

Imbalance between work and life. When a job is located within a house, the boundaries between work and family life may become fuzzier. Some workers may discover that work increasingly intrudes on their personal lives, which can cause burnout and reduced morale.

More meetings are required. The presence of staff across the globe will necessitate some level of ongoing supervision; this may necessitate holding regular virtual meetings. While internet meetings are less disruptive than face-to-face meetings, they are seldom the peak of the workday. Additionally, too frequent meetings might make workers frustrated.

Managing your virtual team

Now onto the actual management of your remote or in any case hybrid team.

Be clear about your expectations.

When talking with your remote workforce about productivity standards, it's crucial to establish clear expectations. Certain productivity expectations may change depending on the work and other factors. You should analyze and record each of these standards separately, this will assist you in identifying tendencies that require attention. It will also assist you in identifying exhaustion or the need for extra training.

Pay close attention to micromanagement.

You could feel more compelled to "check-in" on projects more frequently if you manage projects remotely. However, you must establish a degree of trust with each member of your team in order to successfully lead them successfully. When you have team members who work remotely, you won't be able to monitor them as closely as you would if you had them in the office, but it doesn't imply they aren't doing their tasks. If you can't trust them,you should either review your recruitment decisions or the event that led to your loss of faith in them

Micromanagement can be quite damaging. What you see as proactive project management efforts may appear to a remote worker as toxic micromanagement, hence, you have to be careful and seek clear ways for your team to express their preferences.

Assess the needs of your team.

Being a remote leader requires you to be perceptive and flexible enough to accommodate the needs of the direct reports on your team. Using the abilities you gained from chapter two "knowing your team", you should be able to determine the strengths, weaknesses, and requirements of the members of your team. Some team members require constant validation, some prefer autonomy, and some want more or less contact from their boss. To better understand their preferences you might consider asking the employee how they want to be led, you should inquire about and accommodate their preferences. The goal of outstanding leaders after all, is to eliminate confusion.

Provide your team with the necessary tools and resources

Your remote workforce requires the same access to certain resources as your onsite team does, such as policy and procedure manuals, presentation templates and materials, company laptops, reliable internet access, use of co-working facilities, access to office materials, etc.

It is your responsibility as a manager to make sure that your remote staff has access to these and all other necessary tools. You might need to conduct a brainstorming session with your team members to come up with solutions to this need for an easier transition to telecommuting.

Encourage casual conversations

Working remotely naturally leads to a lot of work-related chats with coworkers; it may take some extra work to replicate popular water cooler conversations, but it's crucial to promote social contacts. Encourage your remote team members to stay in touch with you and the rest of the team frequently. To achieve this, set out a few hours each week for social calls with any employee in the organization. When possible, look for team-building activities that will involve both on-site and off-site staff.

Asynchronous Communications.

Never undervalue one-on-one interaction. Asynchronous communication is beneficial and essential. Calls or messages could be used for this. Joining a Zoom video call can sometimes be much more beneficial. Regular Ask Me Anything (AMA) sessions can be planned so that team members can get to know you as a new leader, discover more about an existing team member, or understand a recent change.

Communicating effectively with your remote team

With communication being a very crucial aspect of leading a remote team,we will treat it separately. This section will arm you with the strategies for communicating properly with your team as well as how to overcome some certain communication challenges you might face.

Communication is crucial when working with a remote team; this cannot be stressed enough. What makes it more difficult is that its requirements are completely different from those of an in-person team at work. When working remotely, teams frequently encounter unique communication obstacles. As a manager, you must comprehend the complexities and difficulties of effective communication in a remote team.

The absence of physical cues, which frequently serve as messages to other team members about limits and preferences, is one of the largest barriers to efficient communication in remote teams. Finding the ideal level of communication—not too little, not too much—might just be challenging.
There are varieties of communication tools, therefore it could be challenging for workers to prioritize messages and tasks arriving from different channels and from team members who aren't using those channels with the same expectations.

Synchronous communication is challenging and occasionally avoided due to slow internet and network concerns. It can be uncomfortable to stay on a call when video chats are malfunctioning or team members are talking over one another, according to participants.

Individuals may have varied ways they would want to receive and exchange information; some may favor visuals, while others may prefer vocal or even written communication. This variety of preferences for information distribution methods may also be a threat.

Micromanagement is also present. You may find yourself closely monitoring, managing, and reminding your team members at every opportunity. As a manager who is used to seeing people in the office if they are performing their tasks properly. You might start to over-communicate and find yourself asking for status updates, checking in on workers frequently, or offering advice that disrupts workflow.

Then, how do you handle these difficulties?

Make a detailed plan for remote work communications.

Setting up a communications plan is crucial for the success of any form of a remote working environment. Finding a unified platform that can meet all of your communication and collaboration demands should be your first step. Your strategy for communicating with employees about remote work should center on informing them of the policies; encouraging attendance at meetings; supporting digital teamwork, etc.

You can utilize a unified digital workplace to make it better because it has all the features and analytical tools you'll need to make sure your remote work communications plan is successful.

Keep your communication as concise and clear as you can.

Your messages may frequently come out as unpleasant, terse, or simply insensitive if there are no verbal or visual indicators, such as body language or facial expressions, to help the recipient understand the context.

Try to use as few words as possible to convey the message's purpose. Your team members should be able to grasp your messages without them being too complicated or wordy.

You must carefully consider your message's tone before sending it. Emojis can be used to improve the clarity, humanization, and overall tone of your message.

Deal with any communication issues in hybrid teams.

When hybrid teams are involved, remote work communication can become exceedingly complicated.

Due to the varied time zones and dealing with team members' delayed reactions, remote workers may not have the same privilege that is enjoyed by onsite workers.

By implementing initiatives like buddy programs and get-togethers where remote and in-office employees may engage and build greater rapport that will result in enhanced communication, you can easily close this communication gap.

Dedicated technologies for synchronous and asynchronous communication should be available to remote teams.

You should continue using instant messaging programs for asynchronous communications, and for synchronous communication such as team meetings and one-on-one conversations, use a video program.

The majority of communication tools have overlapping features, so even if you try to designate distinct tools for various sorts of communication, things can still get complicated.

Some of your staff members could feel pressured to use your instant messaging tool's video calling feature rather than using a different video calling application since it has that capability. Similar to this, team members may prefer to converse about some project-specific aspects rather than using the project management platform, which almost always creates conflict among team members.

In this case, you can manage all of your synchronous and asynchronous communication in one location by using a unified digital workplace platform as opposed to using hundreds of different communication platforms.

With a digital workspace, you can set up specific channels for communication, chat in real-time with your team members, and handle all project-related interactions with ease. Besides, eliminating the need to pay subscription fees for many communication platforms, not only reduces your business expenses but also helps distant teams communicate more effectively and efficiently. It becomes simpler for remote workers to communicate with coworkers and always be informed.

Chapter Eleven: Review

Which values did you think were particularly important to have if you want to lead a remote team successfully?

_____

_____

_____

How do you solve the frequent communication issues that arise when working remotely?

_____

_____

_____

What other challenges do you think you might face while managing a remote team?

_____

_____

_____

How do you intend to deal with these challenges?

_____

_____

_____

Chapter 12: Managing Social Media in Your Setting

When it comes to access to social media, as a manager you need to decide well in advance what you will tolerate, what you will encourage, and what you will prohibit.

While many companies have a policy on social media, the reality is that it is ever-changing. And no sooner is one social media platform felled before another pops up in its place.

Although Internet giants such as Google, Apple, Meta, Microsoft, Amazon, and so forth, are going nowhere fast, today's social media can easily become tomorrow's museum piece. To illustrate this, just consider the diverse fates of the following social media websites that all launched between 2002 and 2005: Friendster, Skype, LinkedIn, MySpace, Facebook, Flickr, Bebo, Reddit.

Accordingly, as I sit here writing this book I have simply no idea whether TikTok, YouTube, SnapChat, Twitter, Instagram, WhatsApp, Telegram, and Facebook Messenger will withstand the test of time.

As a result, in the following discussion regarding *managing social media in your setting,* specific social media platforms will not be named. Rather, we will explore any potential benefits or risks it may present to the team.

Finally, we'll examine whether team members—including you, as the team manager can discuss work on social media.

Use of social media in the workplace

Balance is essential in life, as it is in most things. While you don't want your staff to spend all day on social media, outright banning it could make you seem too cautious. To be fair, your employees will probably still find a way to access it.

Instead of taking social media use at work as a poison, why don't you wield it as an antidote? Asides from boosting morale and allowing employees to take a much-needed break, social media can help with the overall productivity of your team if well managed.

The very many ways social media use can benefit you include;

Morale and employee engagement

In so many ways, allowing your team to use social media at work can promote their engagement and boost morale. It conveys your confidence in them and because of this they will feel appreciated.

Taking frequent, brief pauses will improve your mood and that of your team members, in essence, allowing team members to check social media can make them happy. Also, your team members are more likely to be effective, sociable, and devoted if they are content.

Branding

Social networking is a fantastic tool for spreading goodwill toward your business.

Depending on the type of company you work for, your employer's brand may benefit from encouraging your staff to use social media by sharing behind the scenes updates (think setting up an author signing event for your publishing company, or an update from a trade stand your company is at) about the business, or even funny job posts from your HR department.

I watched a recent Tiktok video which was only less than 30 seconds long. It was a funny ad for a 5 star hotel who was looking for new staff. The video went viral and was seen by hundreds of thousands of both positional customers and new staff members.

In a similar vein, it's an excellent tool for winning over current and new customers.

All of that cannot occur if social media is outlawed completely. Social media is an incredibly powerful tool, and harnessing it in a creative way can both help your business and add a great sense of satisfaction and a new level of creativity to your colleagues who can suggest ideas for new social media strategies.

In fact, some of your employees who do not work in your marketing department, may actually be extremely successful personally on social media and those would be great skills to harness for your business.

Personal development

I firmly believe that social media may aid (committed) employees in honing their abilities. Various articles about how to improve various things are available on some social media networks. The devoted worker may cut through the clutter and immerse themselves in information to grow and prosper.

There are however downsides to it as well, if unmanaged properly social media use at work can cause some of these;

Misuse

Whatever your opinions on using social media at work may be, it's relatively safe to say that if you do permit it, some time will be spent.

The temptation for employees to glance or respond to a passing comment is simply too great. Although most individuals won't notice much of this time wastage, some might. It is up to you to decide whether you think your workers can resist that temptation.

Viruses

Of course, there is also the chance of technological failure. These days, scams, viruses, and hacking are all too common, and a sizable number of them start on social media.

It can be a very large risk to take if you don't have solid security and/or if your crew isn't extremely computer literate.

Mistakes

Of course, social media has the power to both strengthen and utterly demolish your brand. Employees might make mistakes by posting wrong or unacceptable information that can harm the image of your team and brand entirely.

Additionally, it's not always the fault of an employee who makes a mistake and posts something stupid; the act of posting on social media in and of itself may irritate your customers. They might believe you're wasting your time on social media rather than completing necessary tasks.

Bullying and harassment

Knowing personal information about one another can encourage and promote bullying.

Social media is an open platform for people to pick on one another, and even while your staff members might not do it outwardly, they might use what they discover to bully and make fun of coworkers.

Since it's not advisable to completely outlaw social media in the workplace, at the very least, some guidelines or restrictions should be in place to control usage there. Going further, we'll provide you with what you need to set social media boundaries

Creating a policy for the use of social media at work.

The obvious step to managing the use of social media is to create a policy.

To make sure your team members use these sites responsibly and restrict their personal use while at work, your policy has to be clear and has to set the necessary boundaries.

Without these guidelines, staff members could unintentionally damage the team's or company's reputation through bad messages or divisive comments.

It is up to you to decide what activities you deem appropriate or inappropriate on your staff's social media accounts. For instance, if one of your employees sees an unfavorable post about your company, they could be inclined to comment. Instead, you can decide to respond to negative comments yourself or through a member of your social media, public relations, or marketing staff. Make sure your social media policy specifies this requirement.

Even while you have little influence over how an employee chooses to represent themselves on their personal accounts, giving them expert advice will help them grasp the potential impact social media has on business.

Writing your social media policy with input from your staff is typically the best course of action. Maintaining a cheerful attitude and avoiding focusing on sanctions for wrongdoing are also wise moves.

The policy shouldn't be overly restrictive so that employees can effectively represent the organization.

A simple social media policy for a workplace should cover;

- Guidelines for appropriate personal social media use as well as those that relate to the company's use of social media for business purposes. For instance, the company's marketing and PR goals and practices should be followed in all posts made on its behalf.

- Employees should use extra caution when disclosing proprietary or sensitive information or participating in conversations that can damage their reputations or the reputation of the team.

- Whether the business will use its authority to examine and keep an eye on employees' online behavior

- Recommendations for how to respond to clients and the public on social media

- Use of social media in both appropriate and inappropriate situations

- Clarifications about the use of business social media profiles concerning intellectual property rights. However, merely drafting a social media strategy for the workplace is insufficient; you also need to make sure that all staff members are aware of it. Because it is crucial to not only develop a policy but also fully explain it to your team.

- Employees who share firm information without fully knowing their team's policy runs the risk of disclosing sensitive or secret information. Staff members must be informed of your expectations, regardless of whether they will be allowed to use social media for personal reasons or only for work-related ones.

Make sure to review how social networking fits into your current policy, how much personal use is allowed, and what remedial measures could be necessary if excessive use becomes a problem.

Create policies for passwords, file-sharing and chat programs, managing professional profiles, and utilizing personal internet during business hours or while using corporate equipment including laptops, company Wi-Fi, company-issued phones, and other devices.

Think about including a manual for resolving PR problems on social media. When a departing employee uploads anything unfavorable on your social media accounts before their access is canceled or when irate customers start venting online, social media PR disasters can occur.

Additionally, it's critical to provide information on how to post on social media in an emergency, such as canceling all scheduled postings.

How can you utilize social media's many advantages at work without having a detrimental impact on worker productivity?

You can avoid being a victim of the well-known forms of employee internet abuse, such as cyberbullying and data theft, by using workplace internet filtering and monitoring software.

With the help of these technologies, businesses may encourage staff members to utilize social media at work while also giving them the power to enact policies if a significant number of employees misuse their access to social media.

To manage various areas of the social media policy, choose the right people. For example, your information technology (IT) specialist may be the point of contact for approving and denying access to the social media account of your company. Give names and phone numbers to any members of staff who might have inquiries.

Chapter Twelve: Review

If allowed, how can you utilize social media to increase the overall productivity of your team?

_____

_____

_____

_____

What threats do you think the use of social media might pose to your team (mention at least 3)

_____

_____

_____

Write measures to tackle each of those threats.

_____

_____

_____

What will you include in your team's policy for the use of social media? (List 3)

_____

_____

Chapter 13: Growing Your Team's Initiative And Innovation

If you look at the leading businesses in any industry, you'll see that they all share innovation as a common value. Successful managers are aware that adopting the same concepts and techniques they have in the past won't get them very far.

Taking the initiative entails identifying opportunities and acting on them. Any productive business needs self-starters who are action takers and finish tasks. When you take the initiative, you approach things intending to get them done effectively rather than merely crossing them off a list. It involves going above and above on the simple duties given, solving problems, and taking on tasks before someone asks you to.

To feed, guide, and motivate this desire into a strategy that benefits the team members and the business as a whole, however, demands a leader who has what it takes. No matter how effective your team is now, there are always ways to improve it and push it to new heights. This chapter will cover how to develop your team's initiative using different tenets;

- Boosting initiative by using performance appraisal... the right way
- Using financial incentives to foster initiative
- How to encourage lateral thinking in your team members to drive innovation
- Recruiting team members who take the initiative will include some suggestions for innovating job profiles, roles, and descriptions.

Boosting initiative by using performance appraisal... the right way

Several duties come with being a manager in any organization, of these duties is performance evaluation. As a manager, you must routinely evaluate team members' performance over a certain period since it is crucial for effectively assessing an employee's abilities, strengths, and weaknesses as well as evaluating if they should receive a pay increase or promotion.

Great managers are aware of how essential employee performance is to the success of their team as a whole. Excellent managers use appraisals to link employee performance to company objectives.

With the appropriate assessment approach, your team members will see a course for their professional & career advancement. Through training and education, they will become stimulated and pushed towards their personal objectives, and have a clear grasp of their roles and expected outputs. What's more, overall team performance will be positively impacted.

When you talk about the struggles and successes of particular team members, These discussions give employees information about their areas of strength and areas for progress, paving the path for employee development. This self-awareness guarantees that your staff will take their performance difficulties more personally and commit to accepting and fixing them. As has been stated, progress begins with awareness. Employees become more responsible for their activities as a result, and they become more motivated to boost their productivity.

How to do it right!

You may use some of these metrics to ensure continuous performance evaluation.

Prepare in advance

As with anything else, an effective assessment system is built on adequate preparation. Preparing ahead of time for an employee performance review ensures that You have a system and procedure in place.

Here are some things you should have with you;

- A copy of the employee's personnel file.
- Records or notes from earlier evaluations (if they are not already in the employee file). Included in this are the objectives and goals you and the employee addressed during the previous review.
- Copies of suggestions (or complaints) from supervisors, colleagues, or clients.
- Sales, productivity, and other performance metrics that are pertinent to the review type you are performing.

You should make a list of potential questions after reviewing all data comments and supporting documents.

Make sure to let the employee know when and how the appraisal will be conducted. This will ensure that the employee is given enough time to prepare properly.

Conduct a 360-degree evaluation

As you are already aware, this strategy incorporates input from several individuals who interact with each employee, thus firmly putting prejudices to rest.

The employee themself is needed to provide their perspective on their function in the team, as well as that of several other coworkers.

This coordinated approach will provide you with a clear insight into an employee's attitude and behavior, it will also aid with self-improvement, which is beneficial for the person.

Make performance standards available.

What is expected of each employee in terms of quality, demeanor, punctuality, sales, and other factors should be detailed in a handbook that explains how your performance evaluation program operates.

This should contain;

- What your review procedure is like and when it will happen.

- What you are expecting from workers and what they should anticipate from you.

- What can result in an employee being dismissed immediately (for example, stealing), and if in other circumstances they will get a formal warning for their personnel file before the threat of being fired is actual.

Constructive criticism

Make sure you are ready to utilize considerate criticism that will uplift rather than undermine any employee before you sit down with them.

Compared to merely stating what a team member did correctly or incorrectly, this kind of communication is far more successful. It demonstrates that you have been attentive intently and lends credibility to your feedback.

Frequent feedback

Employees should get frequent feedback and clear expectations rather than yearly reviews.

These periodic feedback sessions should be planned on a timetable that complements the employee's specific working hours. With a greater understanding of what occasionally occurs and the ability to identify trends in either high or poor staff performance, you can take advantage of them or put an early end to them.

This strategy also enables you to adjust employee performance on a small scale rather than trying to implement significant changes once or twice a year.

Monitor the Effects of Reviews

Consider the objectives you set for every employee performance assessment. Consider whether the performance has improved or whether something has interfered with it. Check to see whether the habits of your staff have changed—have they become more assured? Has employee morale improved or declined at work? and so forth.

If the outcomes of your employee performance evaluations make things worse than when you discovered them, it's time to rethink your review procedure.

Using Financial Incentives to Foster Initiative

Financial incentives provide you an opportunity to reward your staff for accomplishments and provide them with a way to grow professionally. Workers are more motivated to perform well when an incentive is provided.

However, depending on the decisions you make while creating them, the efficacy of these efforts varies greatly. To put into place efficient financial incentives to help you accomplish your target result you should keep these in mind.

Be specific about your goals.

You must be extremely specific about what you want individuals to be able to perform or achieve when using incentives. There should be no ambiguity on the specifics of what participants must do to achieve the goals. If results are poorly defined, people will constantly try to "play" the incentive game or distort it.

Pick a reward system.

Take into account the opinions and suggestions of your teammates when deciding on the most suitable type of reward system. To ensure that the goals and obligations are spread evenly, it is important to seek suggestions from participants whenever you can during the design process.

Reconsider any incentives that are currently in place. Decide on prizes that are effective and applicable to everyone, and get rid of outmoded or unnecessary incentives.

Create a plan that includes everyone

Include incentives for every level of employment where employees may receive rewards in the entry-level, mid-level, and senior-level positions.

Choose a performance measurement method.

Determine the important measures that demonstrate advancement, improvement, or accomplishment when adopting new incentives so you can determine when teams and individuals succeed. Take into account a range of incentives at different levels of achievement. For higher goal levels, you might designate a higher level of reward.

Make sure there is also clear notification regarding the required minimum performance.

Encouraging Lateral Thinking in Your Team

Lateral thinking employs a new strategy, it provides you with special viewpoints that you wouldn't otherwise be able to see.

It however requires effort to develop lateral thinking on an individual basis inside your team. To promote a "free thinking" culture within your firm without anarchy erupting as a result of rogue individuals, you must be quite flexible.

Since leadership is based on having a clear vision and coming up with solutions, you as a leader should be able to promote a culture of lateral thinking.

Lateral thinking is a skill that can be developed, even though some people are naturally good at it. Here's how to develop it within your group.

Develop the practice of rephrasing difficulties

Start by developing the habit of rephrasing difficulties rather than immediately using time-tested solutions. "Lateral thinkers might discover fresh possibilities that others might not be able to envisage by pushing limits and norms. They naturally look for fresh approaches to challenges. When it's combined with a setting that values invention, creativity, and problem-solving, the lateral thinking strategy works better.

Therefore, you should avoid letting a team meeting devolve into a step-by-step procedure when you're trying to solve a complex problem. Challenge the initial assumptions that were made regarding the issue. Consider finding inspiration in fields unrelated to your own. You can even Invite participants from other teams to the conversation.

Frequently ask questions

During meetings, it's important to ask lots of questions to get your staff to think creatively. Ask your team members to examine problems from various perspectives, this will improve their creative thinking abilities.

Don't simply follow the usual suspects when you're asking questions. Remember that some team members are introverts who might not talk much but may have insightful things to say when asked, be sure to question them as well. Diverse viewpoints are crucial for developing lateral thinking.

Pay attention without judgment.

You should be receptive to hearing suggestions made by workers without prejudice.

It's crucial to recognize your blind spots and try to listen to what your team has to say with as much openness as you can.

Encourage your employees to work from a variety of locations.

If you conduct an off-site meeting or use a hybrid work model that enables individuals to work from different locations at different times, don't undervalue the impact of doing so. encourage your staff to work from various locations throughout the day rather than at the same desk.

Pay attention to employees who take the initiative. Reward and confirm the positive traits you want to see in other people. For people to understand what you value in your staff members, acknowledge initiative both in private and in public. provide both immediate and long-term incentives for anyone who takes initiative. These key motives might include things like greater opportunities for the team or individual growth and advancement or annual bonuses.

Innovative job descriptions and profiles to draw self-starters to your company.

As you are undoubtedly aware, a job description is a document that details the duties and responsibilities of a certain position as well as the education and skills necessary to fill it. Even while it makes it simpler and quicker to connect with the sort of individuals you want to hire, this one crucial step—creating a job description—is sometimes undervalued.

Hiring high-performing workers who take initiative commences with recruiting the right individuals. you need a compelling job description that encourages the ideal applicants to apply to make it feasible.

There are a few essential components that all job descriptions should contain, even though the content will vary depending on the role

Job title and location.

Candidates must immediately understand the position for which they are applying and the location of that position, so be sure to include both information boldly in your job description (ideally in the title or header).

Job description.

As an example, "business manager" or "sales representative" are fairly generic titles—and, depending on the organization, can mean various things—and don't always give applicants a clear idea of the role. Because of this, it's crucial to include a concise outline of the work in your job description. You should also provide any practical details about the position that candidates may need to know (for instance, is the position full- or part-time).

Important obligations.

All of the work obligations, responsibilities, and daily activities that the recruit will be handling should be explicitly stated in your job description.

Job requirements.

The qualifications that candidates must meet to be considered for the position, such as any necessary work experience, competencies, or other talents you're seeking in a candidate (such as the required number of years of experience).

Information about compensation.

Depending on your bargaining style, you could decide to delay providing the salary range upfront, but that doesn't mean you can't mention additional financial incentives, such as overtime compensation, bonus possibility, or any other bonuses. Include in your job description any financial incentives you think may entice prospects to work for you.

Data about the company.

Information about the organization should be included in your job description as well as details about the position. Include any information about your company's work environment, culture, and employer brand that potential employees could find useful or interesting, as well as any information that will draw their attention.

Application guidelines.

Make sure you offer information on how people may apply for the post because the entire purpose of a job listing is to draw applicants for the position.

Now that we have seen what a basic job description should contain, what's next is how to write it such that it attracts mostly the ideal candidates.

Useful tips

Keep things brief and straightforward.

A good job description should be succinct, appealing, and give an outline of the goals of your business. Lessen your concern about the procedural components of the work and concentrate on the important elements that will attract the ideal individuals to the position, such as your fundamental values and success skills. You wouldn't want to create a job description that is overly detailed and lengthy. Candidates could feel confused by the list of prerequisites.

Be original and creative!

As a manager seeking to recruit innovative team members, it's only fair that you are too. You may stand out and attract a candidate's interest if you are willing to welcome new, creative touches.

Asking for a one- to two-minute video from an applicant could be better than asking for a cover letter. For greater comprehension, you may also make a video where you describe the position.

Indicate your values.

Job searchers want to know if they will be able to contribute significantly to your business. If you're seeking individuals that are self-starters and who can contribute their ideas, That has to be mentioned.

Include in your job posting if you have a collaborative work environment that allows applicants to participate in a range of initiatives. Advertise it if you want applicants who are willing to put in the work and bring their own imagination and enthusiasm.

Reassess your business culture

You may advance your hiring strategy and increase your chances of finding the best people for your vacant roles by reassessing your promoted business culture.

Ask current workers for their opinions on the tone, vocabulary, and degree of information used in job descriptions. If your job descriptions accurately represent both the organization's culture and the reality of the market, you'll be more likely to find suitable individuals.

Chapter Thirteen: Review

What 4 importance of performance reviews did you note?

_____

_____

_____

List the things you need to be properly prepared before conducting a performance review session

_____

_____

_____

What steps should you take towards implementing effective monetary incentives?

_____

_____

_____

What is your own definition of lateral thinking?

_____

_____

_____

Write from below 6 terms that shows Lateral thinking

_____

_____

_____

Thinking outside the box, step-by- step process,
creative, rigid, flexible, defined path, direct, indirect, unconventional, alteration, reframing.

What 5 things are unique about your company?

_____

_____

_____

Using this template, write the perfect job description that will attract innovative thinkers;

Job Title (In bold letters)

About (write little about your company . Be sure to include the values that are emphasized in your company with a CTA at the end)

Job summary (summarize what the job title means in the context of your organization)

RESPONSIBILITIES: (This should contain a detailed but concise list of roles to be played and the requirements of the job such as level of skills and education)

BENEFITS: (This should include a bulleted list of bonuses and benefits your company offers)

Chapter 14: Different Ways to Deal with Difficulty

Every manager aspires to build cohesive teams that collaborate well to accomplish business objectives; it is a fantastic professional accomplishment to see your team members flourish as individuals and experience success. But as a leader, you must understand that not everything will go as planned and that life is not always easy.

There are challenging times along the route when you're in charge of the growth of your team members and your employees. Conflicts between personalities, a lack of trust, or a misunderstanding of roles are among the common causes of issues. It is your responsibility to see these hiccups and get the team moving again.

You will encounter difficulties and challenges, how you handle them is what matters. In this chapter, some specific challenges will be mentioned alongside how you can tackle them. We will explore some topics on handling difficulty in the workplace including "how and when to let an employee go"

Conflicts

Your team's effectiveness and issue solving are enhanced by the many viewpoints and information that your team members provide. But conflict can occasionally result from a diversity of ideas and viewpoints.

Even in the most engaged of organizations, conflicts will inevitably arise. Conflicts, regardless of their origin, may swiftly affect motivation in the workplace if they are not handled.

For a team to function well, disagreements must be settled quickly, professionally, and with the least amount of disturbance to production. Any organization's success depends on its capacity to handle team disagreements.

You must maintain your composure and attempt to comprehend the various points of view of all parties throughout the process, whether you are a party to the argument or serving as the mediator.

4 different team conflict types

Four kinds of team disputes that are frequent in office settings are listed below:

Task-related disagreements

Task-based disputes happen when team members depend on one another to finish a task or project. When one team member fails to fulfill their portion of the work, it may hinder the ability of the remaining team members to complete their portions on schedule.

Leadership conflicts.

You should be mindful of your own leadership style and how you engage with your team. To take into account the various demands and personalities of your team members, you might need to modify your leadership style.

Workplace clashes.

Because team members have various preferences on how to complete tasks, work style disputes might arise. While some people prefer to work rapidly and move on to the next activity as soon as possible, others prefer to work slowly and deliberately. Recognizing that everyone has a unique work style and finding methods to work together despite those differences is the greatest approach to preventing these kinds of confrontations.

One of the leading causes of team problems is personality clashes. Team member personality differences are what lead to these kinds of confrontations. Working with someone whose personality is different from your own can be difficult. However, it's crucial to make an effort to comprehend their variances and discover how to collaborate peacefully and effectively.

Managing team member conflicts

Take Charge

Conflict frequently begins with little differences that quickly grow, whether it be excluding someone from an email chain, making an offensive personal remark, or starting a flash debate. Therefore, address conflicts yourself rather than leaving them for HR or your team to handle. This demonstrates your serious approach to confrontation and your will to not tolerate negative behavior.

Observe

Conflict might show up in subtle ways, but you can see it by paying attention to how your team members communicate. What to watch out for includes:

- Body language, such as turning away from others or crossing one's arms.

- Facial emotions like a frown or a downward gaze.
- The use of a cutting, contemptuous, or derogatory tone of voice.

The more familiar you are with each team member, the easier it will be for you to pick up on indications and identify stressors that may be there but not visible. Remember that you might need to take into account if opposing values are causing the disagreement in addition to the specifics of the conflict.

Be unbiased and just.

Be cautious to maintain objectivity even if you concur with one or more members of a competing team.

Allow everyone the space and time to express their interpretation of the situation and to reply to any criticism. Each party must get a chance to speak out and be heard.

Assist When Necessary

Don't let certain people control the discussion or intimidate your more reserved coworkers. If one individual is constantly talking over others, Keep your inquiries focused on the individual who is being interrupted.

If individuals continue to interject, kindly request that they wait until their colleague has finished speaking before presenting their viewpoint.

Eliminate Assumptions

Avoid presenting as fact anything that you merely suspect you know or have heard when leading a dispute conversation. It's advisable to use expressions like "As far as I know" or "As I understand it," for instance.

This also leaves up the potential that your comprehension is inaccurate or insufficient. Additionally, it provides a chance for disputing parties to reassert their arguments and clear up any misconceptions.

Be persistent

Team dispute resolution might take some time. Particularly with erratic, conceited, or dominating personalities. Additionally, it might be difficult to interact with shy or uncommunicative employees. Therefore, it's crucial to have patience and endure.

Be composed

It's crucial to maintain composure and professionalism in the face of disagreement. Before trying to resolve the disagreement, take a few deep breaths and relax. Prepare a strategy to end the disagreement before it escalates and things get worse

Communicate (and listen)

Select a location where you may talk about the disagreement privately. It's crucial that all parties engaged get the chance to express their viewpoints and hear from others. To communicate what you need to say while being attentive and empathic, attempt to comprehend how the other person feels.

Create a Plan

Request a list of the steps to be taken to resolve the dispute from the parties. and persuade everyone to stick with this plan. You may create a schedule of events and mark each one off when it is completed. Hold responsible all those who are involved.

Keep in touch

Follow up on the issue to make sure it has been appropriately fixed. For instance, someone can still feel resentful yet not want to prolong the situation. One-on-one conversations can be used to stop previous disputes from coming up again. Additionally, try doing a private team survey to get feedback and identify any unresolved issues.

Problem employees & weak hires

Problematic employees who need to improve their attitudes and behaviors. Problem workers, irrespective of how they are classified, are the misery of any manager's existence and call for special consideration and competence. According to the experts, There isn't a quick fix, pre-written speech, or psychological trick that can miraculously turn a tough employee into someone you can work with.

Hiring the wrong person is one of the most expensive mistakes you can make in a company. But occasionally, despite your best efforts, you simply end up with a bad hire.

When dealing with deeply ingrained human characteristics, you should be somewhat of a black belt in your managerial and personal skills.

When it comes to advice for handling difficult workers, experts provide several solutions addressing various areas of the process. The first piece of advice is simple: keep employees from ever becoming troublesome employees. Although it can seem like fast advice, making it happen takes a manager to put in constant effort.
It is said that while someone may acquire new talent, they cannot be given sensibility, personality, compassion, or a pleasant temperament.

Every team appears to have at least one person that drains their energy, decreases productivity, and irritates other team members through poor attitude, disobedience to the rules, or just plain strange behavior. You understand that you cannot let these issues become worse.

This section describes inappropriate and destructive employee behaviors, outlines the hazards to the company that might arise from the conduct if it is not altered, and offers suggestions for regulating the behavior of those people who display these behaviors at work.

Problematic employee behavior types

A range of employee behaviors might endanger both the organization and others. Examples and broad categories include:

Gossiping. The activity of a person who constantly communicates private or sensational information about others, whether real or not, is generally referred to as gossiping, although it frequently has both positive and negative aspects.

Displaying overall indifference or harshness. This involves being impolite, abusive, and physically assaulting other people. Examples include becoming irate to the point of yelling, smashing things, or slamming doors.

Bullying. Even though bullying can involve impolite behavior, bullies typically adopt less evident strategies to harm other employees, such as social exclusion, condescending or dismissive remarks, and manipulation.

Showing defiance. Insubordination is the deliberate refusal of an employee to comply with a valid and reasonable directive from their employer. This may appear to be a single instance warranting reprimand or termination, or it may appear to be a series of less serious instances slowly eroding a manager's authority.

Bad attendance. Productivity issues may arise if your employee routinely leaves early, arrives late, or misses deadlines. Regardless of whether the employee's disappearance was brought on by personal circumstances, child care concerns, or job unhappiness, they should still be held accountable for adhering to the practice's established attendance policy.

Being forced to interact with a difficult coworker can be awkward and unpleasant.

Dealing with the challenges of problem employees

Use these tips for managing difficult workers.

Monitor improper conduct

To keep an account of what happened, jot down every incident of mediocre performance or worrying behavior. Ensure to put down the time. Aside from aiding you in remembering and referring to particular events, adequate documentation protects your organization if a discharged employee decides to sue the company for wrongful termination.

Pay Attention to Requests

You should engage the difficult employee in a two-way dialogue. Listen to what they say to pinpoint the problem and account for any workplace issues that could be to blame for the poor behavior. Making an employee feel acknowledged and accepted might occasionally help them behave better.

Comment on Behavior, Not People

You must be careful not to become too personal or emotional throughout the conversation. The main goal is to find a solution, not to stir up controversy. It's important to focus solely on the improper or offensive behavior of the employee rather than condemning the employee personally. They may not have been acting in a harmful way on purpose. Uncertainty, fear, or unresolved personal concerns might be the root of it.

Give clear instructions

Managers may find it difficult to provide severe criticism, but it's vital to give concrete instances of the unacceptable behavior combined with a justification for why it's wrong and how it needs to be changed. By concentrating on specific examples, you may minimize the employee's aggression and provide them with the knowledge that will improve their performance at work.

Cooperate to come up with a fix

The ideal result when you talk to a difficult employee about their conduct is that you both collaborate to come up with a workable solution. Determine what the employee requires from you to adjust, and then discuss the wrong conduct and the acceptable behavior. Accept a solution to the issue.

Make a list of expectations.

Be explicit as to what needs to be improved and set a timeframe. Make a thorough plan of action with a due date and a mechanism for success assessment. The plan should be signed by the employee as well as by you. Both of you should maintain a copy of the document so that the employee may use it to execute the plan and you can evaluate performance moving forward.

Set specific penalties

Your strategy for improving a difficult employee may fail if you don't provide clear consequences if the behavior doesn't change within the allotted term.

A formal written warning, being disqualified from receiving bonuses or promotions, or, in more severe circumstances, losing their job, are all potential repercussions. Employees are not likely to behave differently unless doing so would negatively affect them.

Track Progress

Give your workers the time they need to act properly. Throughout that period, monitor their progress and take note of any issues or non-adherence. If required, check in frequently to learn more about how they are adhering to the agreed-upon strategy, and take appropriate action if they veer off course. After the time frame from your plan has elapsed, arrange a full in-person review to discuss how the circumstance has evolved.

Speak to the HR Department

Set up meetings with the human resources staff to explore the issue. They can help you comprehend the paperwork you require, guide how to deal with inappropriate behavior, and set up a strategy for handling the employee. All business rules and practices for handling difficult workers and, if required, terminating their employment shall be known to HR.

Recognize Hopeless Circumstances

Practically, there will be times when it is impossible to influence an employee's actions in a way that would improve the team's morale and output. If your previous interventions didn't have the desired effect and the individual won't change their conduct, you must adhere to your company's termination procedure to limit your losses.

This leads us to the daunting topic "terminating employees"

Terminating Employees

You will despise firing people, just like 99.9% of all other leaders on the earth. Although it's the most unpleasant aspect of the job, leadership inevitably involves it.

Even if an employee has been unpleasant, rude, and uncooperative to your leadership, it may still be tough for you to fire them. However, you should be aware that allowing such behavior to continue in the team will not only foster a negative atmosphere for you and the other team members, but it may also lead to others questioning your leadership skills, lower workplace morale, or endanger the health or safety of the other team members.

If your doubts persist, you might have to reconsider your rationale. It's critical that you have a reason in mind. Remember that you must follow all applicable state and federal laws when firing an employee.

You can dismiss an employee based on the following criteria:

- Problems with performance
- Concerns with attendance or persistent tardiness
- Criminal activity or stealing
- Threats or acts of violence against team members
- Company restructuring
- Inappropriate character or attitude

Although you have the option to fire an employee for either of these factors, your ultimate choice should be based on the specifics of each situation and the individual employee.

You must complete all of the procedures in the preceding section "dealing with challenges of problem employees" before you make the significant decision to fire an employee.

Don't let someone go without first reviewing their performance. Be careful not to surprise your employee. Make sure that they receive performance evaluation and the appropriate coaching prior to being fired. This not only gives them a warning but also enables you to uncover a possible basis to terminate them and pinpoint the root of their failure.

Once you have a solid justification for firing an employee, make your choice and take action right away, in consultation with your HR department. It's preferable to stop it as soon as you can since the reason you're terminating them probably has to do with the impact they're having on the business or your workers.

Knowing the right way to terminate someone's job might speed up the procedure. Abiding by the right procedures when firing an employee helps the individual accept the decision and safeguards your business from future legal action.

After the previous warning and organizing your reasons, the first step is to get everything ready in advance.

To ensure the procedure goes as smoothly as possible, practice the words you intend to use while speaking with the employee and have all the necessary paperwork ready. Bring all relevant communication you've had with the employee throughout their employment, including performance reports and written warnings. This enables you to examine them and collect evidence to support your decision to terminate their employment. Make a transitional document that outlines key information about their termination.

You must, at the very least, be clear about the following steps, such as the employee's last day of work, last payment, benefits, continuing projects, remaining vacation days, etc. Before the meeting ends, make sure everything is agreed upon and that they have the necessary information. The employee in issue will be required to sign the termination paperwork during a meeting you will schedule later.

Make a list of talking points if you worry that your anxiety will get in the way.

Pick the right moment and location.

The termination meeting should be held in a quiet area, such as your office. The employee should be treated with respect and the discussion should be held in a quiet setting because it is a delicate subject. Make the termination meeting during a time of day when it is calmer. Wait till the conclusion of the employee's workday when there are fewer people present before firing them. This keeps out nosy onlookers and pointless inquiries.

Before firing an employee, arrange a face-to-face meeting with them.

Wait till you have a face-to-face meeting before firing an employee rather than doing it over the phone, in a letter, an email, or even a phone conversation. You must show them respect even though you are ending their position. It's crucial to let them go in a way that preserves your relationship with the rest of your staff.

Go with a witness.

Don't dismiss a worker by yourself... You never know how someone would respond since firing is a sensitive and delicate affair. Have a second employee attend the termination meeting to prevent a potential job termination dispute. They can speak up when you run out of things to say in addition to acting as a witness. Think about bringing a human resources representative with more expertise in firing workers. They can steer the conversation in the right direction and guarantee that the employee is treated fairly, equally, and professionally by drawing on their expertise. If you don't have a specialized HR team, just make sure you're in the room with someone else you can trust when the firing occurs.

Keep the dialogue brief.

You don't need to express your unhappiness since the employee has received performance reviews and comments that let them know they're falling short of expectations. Since most employees want to know why they were fired, create a succinct response that doesn't go into too much detail or assign blame. Instead of describing all the ways they've failed, just say that you've previously talked to them about their performance concerns and that you're letting them go because their work isn't up to par with the company's expectations for that job.

Make sure employees are aware that you have decided to end employment.

Don't let them believe that it isn't a definite choice. Don't give them the impression that you are open to changing your opinion. Ensure that you have well-thought-out grounds to fire them before setting up the termination meeting.

Avoid a negative conclusion.

Consider concluding the meeting on a good note and encouraging them to advance in their career. Sending them off with words of support demonstrates your continued regard for them. Wish them the best of luck in their future undertakings and in a job that is more suitable for them. You might also underline that, given their many qualities, you are confident they will find another opportunity to pursue.

Modify logins and security account information.

Even if you no longer provide them access to your business's systems, be careful to update the passwords, computer logins, and entry codes as an extra precaution. Changing this information stops them from doing anything maliciously, like logging in and stealing data from your company, if they are still angry over being fired.

Designate a person to accompany the employee out.

Have someone accompany them while they pack their personal belongings, and then have that person retrieve their keys and personal ID card and walk them out of the building.

Self evaluation.

Make a self-evaluation. If you've reached the point where you must terminate someone, now is a great time to assess your hiring, supporting, and developing methods. Do you observe a trend here? If so, you should deal with the underlying reasons for your people management problems.

Chapter Fourteen: Review

What are the possible types of conflicts that can ensue in the workplace?

_____

_____

_____

What 5 steps can you take to control the situation in the case of a conflict between team members?

_____

_____

_____

Mention 2 problematic employee behaviors

_____

_____

_____

How do you deal with an employee that exhibits any
of those two?

_____

_____

_____

What do you do when every effort to change an
employee proves futile?

_____

_____

_____

On what criteria should you fire an
employee?(mention 4)

_____

_____

_____

Chapter 15: Cultivating Great Traits for Continuous Growth

Additionally, managers must always improve. Your success as a manager will have a direct impact on how well your team operates because you are charged with managing others and educating and directing the team.

It is just difficult for anyone to move a team forward if they are at a standstill. It's helpful for you to reflect on your strengths and weaknesses in the same way that you evaluate the performance of your team members.

There are many leadership qualities that characterize excellent managers, but this chapter will assist you in identifying the abilities and qualities you should have to support the development of both you and your team.

Improving yourself

The most effective managers work hard to acquire the abilities that will enable them to lead well. By reading this book, you already possess this quality. You are taking the necessary action to develop your potential and act as an example for your team by putting the ideas taught in this chapter into practice.

There are many areas where you may improve, therefore I advise you to assess whether you already possess enough of the abilities and characteristics that will be covered below.

If you already have these abilities, you can work on honing them; if not, congratulations—you now do.

Preserving composure under stress

Everyone experiences pressure, regardless of position, profile, title, experience, or gender; being a manager does not absolve you from it; in fact, it may occur frequently.

Whether the pressure is coming from you, from those in your organization who are above you, from your coworkers, or from the circumstance itself, it's stressful. There may be pressure because you have a lot to do or because expectations have been placed on you. Your actions in these situations will have an impact on how your coworkers and employees remember you. When a leader falters, so may their followers, which hinders productivity and reduces morale.

Maintaining your composure as a manager has numerous advantages for both you and your staff,

A competent manager who maintains composure in stressful situations is more likely to inspire trust in their team. Maintaining your composure under pressure not only teaches your staff to rely on you but also helps you win their loyalty.

You can think more clearly and more calmly if you can control your emotions. Because you can think things through properly, you don't rush into things and make mistakes.

A great manager who has developed their abilities doesn't jump to conclusions; rather, they consider decisions more carefully before making them, comparing and contrasting many scenarios and solutions to guarantee they make the best choice.

How can you teach yourself to remain composed in the face of extreme stress?

Maintaining a healthy lifestyle

Maintaining a healthy lifestyle can help you reduce your stress and remain focused all day at work.

Make sure you get a decent night's sleep, engage in some exercise, and consume healthy meals every day. Give up junk food, and exercise briefly each morning. You'll feel more motivated to take on daily difficulties after doing this.

Set realistic priorities.

Set reasonable goals for yourself, evaluate your to-do list, and rearrange your workload according to the things that are most important. If you feel like your schedule is already busy, setting priorities also provides you with the chance to change deadlines or hire assistance.

One step at a time.

One task at a time approach will not only improve your focus but also enable you to do more tasks.

Instead of multitasking, concentrate on what you are doing at the moment. Don't give in to the impulse to stress about the upcoming task on your list. You may even pledge yourself that you will always complete one task before moving on to another.

Take a brief rest

Between chores, take a brief rest to clear your mind and recharge your batteries. Consider taking a 15-minute walk outside if you can to get some fresh air. Take advantage of this opportunity to think about topics other than work.

Consider your feelings.

You need to give yourself time to absorb your feelings before you can relax. Consider why you're stressed and find a solution rather than ignoring your stress levels. You could either ask for a delay in this situation or check if a teammate can assist.

Use deep breathing exercises

When your breathing becomes labored, take a little break from your work to catch your breath. In a peaceful area, close your eyes and concentrate on your breathing. Deep breathing exercises can calm your mind and make you feel more at peace, even if you only spend a short while doing them.

Consider the positive rather than the bad.

Focusing on the advantages might make you feel better about fulfilling your duties while you're under pressure. You might persuade yourself that difficulties are advantageous circumstances for your career by viewing difficulties as chances to develop. You can develop a naturally positive outlook over time.

Set limitations.

Don't overwork yourself; set some limits for yourself. To be in a better mental state when you eventually have time to start filling your schedule once more, you can aim to finish the tasks on your present to-do list before taking on any new ones.

Distribute your tasks.

Even though you are the manager, you are not expected to manage everything by yourself. Depending on who can handle them, decide which chores you can assign to others. In the end, delegation reduces your workload and makes it easier for you to complete other chores and administrative responsibilities in a calmer state.

Overcoming Resistance

Employees can easily become the biggest opponents of change, despite the fact that change is ongoing and unavoidable. While carrying out your duties as a great manager, you discovered a new and better way to approach project execution or there is a new company policy that you are to enforce in your team. You announce it to your team, but they do not react with the expected glee; in fact, they may even start arguing against your ideas.

This shouldn't surprise you because it happens all the time, especially when people don't accept the change, have no faith in the leadership, or think the new project is necessary. Employees occasionally may believe that a different change is required or they may have developed cynicism as a result of several failed change attempts. They could believe that this is just another "flavor of the month" idea that will soon fizzle out. Some folks simply don't like change very much.

You can make use of these to battle and lessen team resistance;

Determine the cause of any resistance.

Understanding the cause of resistance is the first step toward overcoming it. Pay close attention to warning indications like complaints or outright rejections of new efforts. Understanding why your employees are pushing back in the first place is even more crucial than recognizing when resistance is becoming an issue. The following are the common fundamental reasons for resistance:

- Lack of understanding of the changes being made and Fear about the effects of the changes on employment roles
- Failed attempts at change in the past
- Lack of dedication and support from previous managers
- Fear of losing a job

You may more effectively decide how to address resistance to change by understanding why employees are doing so.

Inform the team members about the change through communication.

Employees' resistance to changes will be reduced by communication and education about them, which will also help them understand how these changes might benefit them. Make sure to educate your team members and provide them with all the information they require before implementing any change at all. Utilizing the communication techniques you learned in chapter 2, make sure that each person receives enough information to create wise judgments.

Involve them in the design process.

Team members' doubts about the organization's skills may lead to opposition to change on their part. It is imperative that you involve your team in the change's design. Team members will be involved in the change, the identification of potential problems, and the development of solutions through a collaborative effort. Team members are less inclined to oppose a strategy they helped create.

Change properly the first time.

Employee perception of future projects will be negatively impacted by failed attempts to alter organizational behavior. If you're going to change something, be sure you're taking all the necessary steps to assure its success and establish reasonable deadlines. Don't overwork your employees or demand almost immediate satisfaction. One statistic sums up the realities of change management: It takes time.

Support

Impatience might result from the routine changes brought on by organizational transformation, especially if team members are not accustomed to stepping outside of their comfort zone. A good leader must cultivate emotional intelligence and connect with their followers. Now is the time for you to show them that you are behind them.

Making facilitated discussion groups where you encourage people to address their concerns or even let out their anger is a terrific approach to show your support. This will make it clearer to you what kind of support each person requires.

Delegating

We recognize that you have only recently made the change and that moving from doing to leading may not come naturally to you. You can get away with "rolling up your sleeves" for the first few times, but you must understand that eventually, your responsibilities will get more difficult. By expanding your presence through the actions of others, you optimize your leadership potential.

You must motivate your team to put their best efforts toward your shared priorities. Don't let your attention to detail prevent you from focusing on the bigger picture of leading. By assigning duties to your team, you are able to generate significant profits. Free up your time so you can concentrate on tasks that will expand the business and produce the maximum profits.

You must understand that you cannot accomplish everything alone; this is why a team is formed. Your role is to LEAD and MANAGE people, not to carry out their tasks. Share the responsibility, assign projects, and help your staff members grow in knowledge and proficiency. Given your endorsement, they might pleasantly surprise you.

Delegating increases open communication and trust in addition to lightening your workload and allowing you more time for important things. You will gain enormously if your team feels trusted and free to communicate with you. A successful team is based on open communication and trust.

Employees appreciate it when their managers delegate to them, thus delegating has benefits for both you and your team. Most people see this as a sign that they are respected and trusted employees who are capable of greater achievement. This may inspire employees more than any pizza party for the team ever could.

Team members can become very creative and very motivated to achieve if they feel free to carry out assigned responsibilities in their own unique style. Their individual initiative and drive to accomplish the objective you have set before them can result in outstanding outcomes. The status and acclaim that come with making a difference will be cherished by your team. They will feel proud and accomplished for having made a major contribution.

Delegating work to your employees and assisting them in developing new abilities not only benefits them but also provides your firm with staff that is more competent and better trained. It creates a culture of passion, invention, creativity, cooperation, and openness while fostering trust, boosting morale, and promoting high production and efficiency. It will lower staff turnover and give the company staff that is better qualified and more skilled.

Some managers mistakenly believe that delegation equates to assigning tasks, therefore they avoid doing it, squandering their own time as well as the time and resources of the organization. You are a great manager, not just any manager, and you understand the value of delegation. It's a sign of a strong leader rather than a weakness.

Here are some suggestions to assist you with delegation so that your team can divide the effort and create progress that is advantageous to everyone.

Understand what to delegate

Delegation is the process of removing tasks from your plate that you shouldn't be performing, not shifting them to someone else's. It's crucial to understand the distinction. For instance, you should address any personnel issues or performance evaluations. However, some daily tasks don't need your supervision. Is there a task that you consistently take on even if you know your colleague is more qualified to finish it? Would giving the project to another employee advance their professional interests? Delegate if someone else could complete the task more effectively or if you believe this is an opportunity to learn. While providing you time to concentrate on more strategic issues, it will demonstrate to your team that you value and trust them.

Play to the Goals and Strengths of Your Employees

Understanding the talents, limitations, and preferences of your team members is a key component of being an effective leader. Don't provide a task that needs a lot of cooperation to someone who strongly enjoys working alone rather delegate to someone that enjoys collaboration. For other tasks, someone on your team probably possesses the specialized knowledge required to produce the desired outcome. Utilize that and play to the strengths of your team members.

Specify the desired result.

Delegating isn't about throwing work on someone else's plate. The initiatives you transfer to others should be in the right context and have a direct connection to the organization's objectives. Everyone involved in a project should have a clear understanding of the objectives, deadlines, and success criteria before they begin working on it. You should impart fundamental knowledge without meddling in details. Inform staff members of your objectives or the milestones you hope to reach, then let them approach the issue in their own way.

Never strive for perfection. Say something like, 'Here is what we are doing. What we're after is this. Someone else might carry out a task differently than you would, such as "I want you to get the sale," as opposed to "Follow up on those leads." It doesn't matter as long as you find what you're looking for.

Provide the appropriate authority and resources

It is your responsibility as a manager to offer all three if the individual you are delegating work to needs certain authority, resources, or training to execute the task. Establish a communication route so the person you're delegating to feels comfortable asking questions and providing status updates. Make sure the person you're delegating to has the tools and abilities they need to execute the task—or give a mechanism for them to develop those skills.

Giving someone a difficult assignment to do will annoy both of you because your colleague won't be able to accomplish the intended result, and you'll probably need to put that work back on your to-do list.

Be persistent

You most likely have more years of experience in your field as a manager. As a result, an employee may take an hour to perform a work that you may finish in 30 minutes the first time.

Although you might be tempted to complete some things yourself because you know you can do them more quickly, remain patient with your workers. Remember the first time you finished a particular task early in your career. It's likely that you weren't as effective as you are now; your capacity for time management has increased.

You'll observe that the job gets done faster over time as you continue to delegate and your employees grow more familiar with the tasks that need to be completed.

Deliver (and Request) Feedback

After the duties you've outsourced are finished, you should provide feedback to your staff and vice versa in addition to keeping track of progress.

Nothing is worse than a manager giving an employee a task and then blaming them when anything goes wrong. Don't let that manager be you. Don't be scared to offer constructive criticism if a task wasn't finished as required. The next time a similar work is issued, your employees can use this feedback as inspiration and make adjustments.

Give due credit

When someone completes the work or project you assigned to them, express your sincere gratitude and highlight any particular accomplishments.

Making a note of those details provides folks with a guide for what they should continue to do to be successful.

The more you acknowledge and appreciate the people you've assigned tasks to, the more probable it is that they will want to collaborate with you on future tasks.

Sense of humor

A good sense of humor is one of the most desirable qualities in a leader. Even when the situation is unchangeable, jokes may greatly decrease stress and strain. Good managers use humor to release tension and keep difficulties in perspective. Being approachable and having a good sense of humor also helps your team members work more efficiently and stress-free.

Everyone on your team will gain from a little lighthearted humor because it will make the workplace more enjoyable and ultimately increase your bottom line. Humor not only helps people cope with stress but also increases motivation and engagement.

Like a muscle, a sense of humor can be strengthened by regular exercise.

Try to include a humorous element in every speech or meeting; this will make your audience more receptive to you. Try cracking a joke or bringing up a time when you made an embarrassing mistake when you were chatting with coworkers.

Humor is serious business! One of the best management tools is humor, which you absolutely need to have if you want to build great teams, inspire your staff, close more favorable sales, and elevate your social standing. In conclusion, it will advance your career and help you become a better, more effective leader.

Work-life balance

There used to be a clear line between work and home. But in today's world, it is increasingly probable that work may interfere with your personal time, and maintaining a healthy work-life balance is no simple task. Being a manager, You go above and beyond to maintain everyone's happiness and productivity because you are the team-leading champion. It's not always simple, though.

Large initiatives can become time-consuming nightmares that erode personal liberties (and hobbies). This may be especially true if you put in a lot of overtime. Technology that allows for constant connectivity may cause work to invade your personal time. Before you know it, you're experiencing general burnout.

Unbalances between work and life can happen for a number of reasons. At work, this could take the form of higher workloads or receiving challenging jobs. Work and life imbalance problems affect your team too. Your employees' effectiveness, motivation, and productivity will all decline. They then quickly grow aloof and disengaged. It can eventually result in burnout, which can cause a variety of physical and emotional conditions, more absences, and poor productivity.

A competent manager puts their team's health and wellbeing first, and they take the necessary efforts to learn what each team member understands by work-life balance so they can support them in achieving it.

You must first educate your employees before you can start putting work-life balance techniques into practice in your company. Your efforts will be ineffective if they're not devoted to taking time off and recharging.

Here are some things you can do to help yourself and your team effectively balance work and life.

Put quality and task completion first.

You can be tempted to think that success is determined by how much time is put into it, which could lead you to demand greater work hours from your team. However, I want you to know that success is determined more by how well work is done than by how much time is put in. Instead of focusing on your team's total number of hours worked, you should pay attention to the quantity and caliber of work being completed. Allow staff to choose when to work longer hours and when they can afford to leave early or during the day for an appointment as long as doing so is supportive of the needs of end customers. For instance, starting early at 6-2 may not be able to support end users from 2-5 if they require support from 9 to 5.

Equalize workload

Review the workloads on your team, and be sure to spread the work fairly. This calls for a thorough awareness of each team member's skills and the length of time required to do particular jobs; fortunately, you already know this from the chapter. Give employees with insufficient abilities no complex or time-consuming jobs. Assign assignments based on who can complete them the best. Having assigned duties To prevent anyone from being upset or stressed or overly tired, communicate frequently, check in with team members, ask if they're not overburdened, and so on.

Take a break

The body can become refreshed and the mind can become more focused with periodic short rests. Encourage team members to leave their desks and take in some fresh air. It's crucial to give your staff members a change of scenery, especially if they work from home and may feel a little more alone. A quick stroll outside can help you put work-related concerns into perspective.

Promote vacations

Vacations, paid time off, and unscheduled days should all be used for leisure. Not operating (or thinking about working). "Everyone should have the opportunity to unwind and recharge after work. Encourage your teammate to make use of their vacation time. Inform them not to access their work emails during their scheduled downtime.

Give listening ears to family's needs.

Be mindful of team members' childcare needs and make every effort to be accommodating when they ask for time off. The same is true for people who are taking care of parents or other family members. Parental employees frequently struggle to strike a balance between work and life. Try to be sympathetic in your decisions whenever team members request flexible working hours due to family obligations.

To foster a healthier family life for all parents, regardless of gender, ensure that moms and fathers receive equal parental leave and other benefits.

As a manager, set a good example.

It must be reminded again and again that, if you work long hours and never take a break, your staff, being a reflection of you, will do the same. You'll be giving your teams a bad example. To fit in, they will frequently replicate this conduct. Your responsibility is to demonstrate that you prioritize work-life balance by being on time, taking breaks, and avoiding emails after business hours. Your team members follow your example. Your colleagues will assume they should do the same if you send emails at all hours of the day and night or put in long hours on the weekends.

Know the goals that your coworkers are pursuing.

Each team member is a distinct individual with a different idea of what constitutes a healthy work-life balance. It will be easier for everyone to attain better balance if you adjust your strategy to match each person's needs rather than attempting a one-size-fits-all strategy. Find out what you can do to support each employee's goals for work-life balance by having a conversation with them. While some people might profit from converting to part-time hours, others might want to change their regular work schedule. It's crucial to have an open mind and be adaptable.

Use the methods listed above to foster a work environment that values work-life harmony. And use tools to streamline the process.

Body language

Team members can learn a lot from a manager's body language, and it can even affect how they behave and perform. You can make sure you're giving your team members the proper signals of engagement and participation by paying attention to your body language.

Without using words, body language expresses ideas. By observing your body language, people can infer how you're feeling and even what you might be thinking. Your body language, eye contact, posture, facial expressions, and utilization of personal space can all strengthen, weaken, or even undermine your message. Additionally, your team or staff will notice this type of mismatched signal more immediately and critically than virtually anyone else.

You convey mixed signals when your nonverbal cues and verbal cues are inconsistent with one another (for example, breaking eye contact and looking around the room while asserting that you are being honest, or checking your watch when a subordinate is speaking while asserting that you are listening).

Effective managers have certain body languages that makes it easier for them to relate to and befriend their team members and employees.

Communicate as a manager by using these body language tactics.

Match your words and actions

Don't cross your arms or bury your hands in your pockets if you want to promote collaboration since we tend to believe more of what we see than what we hear. Keep your eyes fixed on the speaker when they are praising the promising future of a new product. Don't smile when breaking bad news. In addition, never pay even a fleeting thought to a text or phone call. Leave your phone at your desk or in your bag, whatever is preferable.

Sit straight and tall.

Sit up straight and tall in your seat as opposed to slouching. Extend your arms, legs, and even your possessions into the area around you on purpose.

You can "extend" yourself by putting your hands on the armrests, extending your legs, or placing a notebook on the table. By occupying space, you demonstrate that you are involved, present, and ready to make choices. I'd rather follow than lead, you are expressing when you recline into your chair or withdraw into a corner. Stay upright; don't slouch. Otherwise, you'll come across as drained and unmotivated.

Be accessible.

Your staff may be scared by you if you have a more aggressive personality type that naturally occupies space and effortlessly exudes authority. Your aim should be to make them feel at ease enough to approach you and express their opinions. Avoid pacing, smile gently, and sit down when you can to keep your team calm.

This modifies the atmosphere of the conversation and relieves pressure on the other person, allowing them to unwind, reflect, and regain calm.

Hold your body still.

Never show irritation, worry, or boredom, no matter how you might feel on the inside. Fidgeting, pacing, head nodding, leg twitching, toe-tapping, face caressing, hair pulling, and chair whirling are all signs of poor self-control and will not instill confidence in your team about your leadership skills. If you have a tendency to fidget, try standing with your feet firmly planted and your hands hanging by your sides. Keep your lower body (and the chair) stationary while seated.

Confidence

Lacking self-assurance, people frequently use "self-soothing" body language that isolates them from others. Watch your natural tendencies the next time you are giving a presentation or a one-on-one conversation. Avoid crossing your arms, tying your knees together, putting your hands in your pockets, or wringing your hands while speaking to your staff. These actions reveal a lack of confidence and nervousness. Opening up physically demonstrates both vulnerability and assurance. When you're sitting, keep your knees uncrossed, hands by your sides, shoulders back, and chin up.

Actively listen

Yes, you are busy; you have a ton of stuff to accomplish and a dozen things on your mind. Don't let your "busyness" come across, though, if you've taken the time to speak with someone. Instead, make them feel like they are the center of your universe. This demonstrates empathy and demonstrates that, despite your busy schedule, you still have time to listen to your staff. Make eye contact, cock your head to the side, nod, and adjust your facial expressions to fit the tone of what they're saying as they're speaking. Do not rush when it is your moment to talk. Think about what you've heard while you pause, inhale, nod, and breathe. Once you have intelligently responded, reiterate the main points of what was said.

Keep your facial expressions in check.

Your body language alone has the power to discourage your staff and lessen their chances of success. If you roll your eyes, furrow your forehead, pout, or purse your lips, you are sending a subliminal message. Make sure your face is relaxed by expanding your jaw and relaxing your facial muscles before you enter a meeting with your personnel. Then, during the meeting, maintain a neutral or optimistic demeanor.

Time management

The overall workflow and relationships across teams can be improved with simple time management and productivity tactics.

The inability to prioritize their work and poor time management cause managers to feel overwhelmed, which might cause them to make mistakes or give in under pressure.

Since it is your job to ensure that employees reach their full potential, it is important for you to understand what promotes and deters overall productivity. Additionally, you should be aware of the types of productivity metrics being gathered and how they connect to the short- and long-term objectives of your team.

You may better control your time and productivity by implementing some of the tactics listed below.

Make a list

We can't possibly keep a lot of information in our thoughts. You can create a written reminder by making lists, such as a daily calendar, contacts to call, or chores to finish over a certain period. Set the most urgent issues in order of importance so you know which to work on first. Do not create lengthy or ambiguous lists. rather, create basic, lucid to-do lists.

Prioritize key tasks.

Even if it seems obvious, it bears repeating. Start with the most important duties. Even if a worker performs nothing else that day, they will have succeeded in finishing the crucial tasks they had to.

You must lead the team skillfully and assist them in learning how to prioritize. Team members may find it challenging to focus on crucial duties when the number of tasks increases. They might discover that they multitask and devote less time to more pressing things.

Make sure to steer the staff to the most crucial work and explain the highest priorities to them. They will be able to focus and use their time more effectively if they do this.

Make a schedule and follow it

The list you have made can serve as the schedule's blueprint. Encourage your group to make their own timetables as well. Depending on their level of dedication and the duration of the projects, you should make a timetable for the day, the week, the month, or anything else. The greatest strategy is to have both short-term and long-term objectives. To keep the team engaged and more productive, set out time slots for the planned tasks and activities.

Know when to say "NO"

Teach your team to refuse certain requests. While being able to manage several projects at once is helpful, it's equally crucial to identify when things are getting out of control. When they have too many commitments going on at once, encourage them to decline other tasks so they can concentrate on the most crucial ones.

Execute tasks in groups

Instead of treating them haphazardly, you can use the practice of grouping related jobs together and work on them sequentially. When you're in the zone, it makes sense to approach similar activities because various tasks call for different types of thought.

Optimize meeting interactions

Meetings are crucial since they allow you to monitor the team's progress and ensure that everyone is aware of their responsibilities and assigned tasks. But too many meetings prevent things from getting done. Instead of ceasing meetings Keep them targeted and succinct.

Take distractions away

Make sure staff members give their full attention to the pressing duties at hand. As they finish tasks, they should experience a thorough immersion in their work. A regulation prohibiting the usage of unnecessary phone calls and browser tabs keeps distractions to a minimum when working on a task.

Utilize downtime.

Encourage team members to fill downtime with beneficial pursuits like watching an instructional video on YouTube or listening to a growth-related podcast.

Avoid working long hours and multitasking

Contrary to what many people think, multitasking doesn't make you more productive. Encourage focusing on one activity at a time to solve the issue of employees feeling compelled to put in extra time because they can't do things within the allotted time. Higher performance and greater happiness will result from this.No matter what job route a person may be on, success will always depend on maintaining growth and development. There is always a desire to improve and do more.

It is very simple to forget that every individual, leader or not, has their personal development to consider, being a person comes before being a manager.

One prevalent myth about job advancement is that once someone reaches senior management, their career is done, and they no longer need to advance. In other situations, managers are frequently thought of as having greater professional and personal experience, but this isn't always the case.

Chapter Fifteen: Review

Make a list of all the necessary traits that were discussed in this chapter

_____

_____

_____

List three things you can do to keep yourself calm under pressure

_____

_____

_____

Write three causes of employee resistance

_____

_____

_____

How can you provide solutions to each of these causes?

_____

_____

_____

What does delegating tasks mean to you?

_____

_____

_____

Write three ways delegating tasks can be of benefit to you and your team.

_____

_____

_____

How can you delegate tasks effectively? (List at least 4 steps you can take to achieve this)

_____

_____

_____

Why is a good sense of humor a trait you should possess? (give 3 reasons)

_____

_____

_____

What factors should you focus on to make your humor effective?

_____

_____

_____

List 5 steps you intend to take towards maintaining work-life balance for you and your team.

_____

_____

_____

List 3 time management techniques you have used before.

_____

_____

_____

What 5 time management tips from this chapter do you intend to use?

_____

_____

_____

Conclusion

Phew! It's been one awesome ride. It is exciting that you were able to read till the very end of this book.

Various aspects of being a manager have been explored in this book " First Time Manager" with the aim of arming you with just about everything you need to become a great manager. Through a series of useful tips and step by step guides, practical examples, templates etc. This book has been able to show you how to handle situations using tested and trusted approaches. It is however up to you to utilize what has been written here to take your team to that great height.

Like it was mentioned in the book, becoming a great manager requires improving oneself, you have taken a step to that and you can still do more.

I wish you luck!

And one last note...

Before you go, I have a small request to make. I would really appreciate it if you could review this book and share your lessons learned. Doing so will help me a lot in getting this book out to other managers who can benefit from the tips and strategies I have shared. Thank you!

Enjoy the next book in the series.

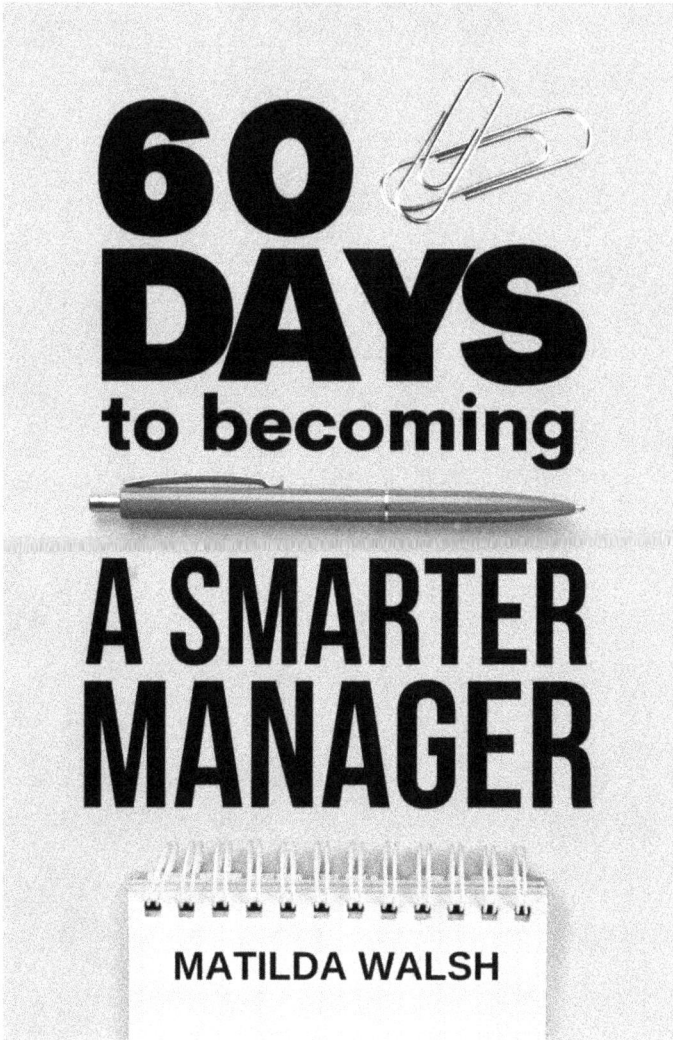

60 DAYS
to becoming
A SMARTER
MANAGER

MATILDA WALSH

www.ingramcontent.com/pod-product-compliance
Lightning Source LLC
Chambersburg PA
CBHW071332210326
41597CB00015B/1430